3.95

Brother Shafi Chowdhury
CHAIRMAN : AL-MUTTAQIIN
62 WEST AVENUE
WALLINGTON SURREY
SM6 8PH ENGLAND
TEL: 0181 - 686 1637

THE RELIGION OF THE SUFIS

From *The Dabistán* of Mohsin Fani

TRANSLATED BY
DAVID SHEA
AND
ANTHONY TROYER

INTRODUCTION BY
IDRIES SHAH

The Octagon Press
LONDON

Copyright © 1979 by The Sufi Trust

Introduction Copyright © 1979 by Idries Shah

No part of this publication may be reproduced or transmitted in any form or by any means, electronic, mechanical or photographic, by recording or any information storage or retrieval system or method now known or to be invented or adapted, without prior permission obtained in writing from the publisher, The Octagon Press Limited, except by a reviewer quoting brief passages in a review written for inclusion in a journal, magazine, newspaper or broadcast.

Requests for permission to reprint, reproduce, etc., to:
Permissions Department, The Octagon Press Ltd.,
14, Baker Street, London W1M 1DA, England

ISBN: 900860 65 0

Published for The Sufi Trust by

The Octagon Press

Printed and Bound in Great Britain by
Tonbridge Printers Ltd., Tonbridge, Kent

CONTENTS

Introduction by Idries Shah   5
Preliminary Discourse by Anthony Troyer   9
The Religion of the Sufis   27

INTRODUCTION

by Idries Shah

It is said, with what truth I do not know, that an editor sending a fledgling reporter to get material on a celebrity for publication in a mass-circulation journal, will brief him thus: "Find out what he has for breakfast, and make sure that you tell the reader how this information will benefit him". Few people in the West have heard of the *Dabistán*. But if you refer to an Eastern book, especially one with a strange name, in the West, you will be likely to get a reaction which perhaps underlines the basic accuracy of the editor's estimate of his public: "Who wrote it? What does the title mean? What use is it to me?"

Nobody knows for certain who wrote it, but it is attributed to Mohsin Fani of Kashmir, who may well have been its author. The title, according to its British co-translator Anthony Troyer, means "The School of Manners". He also thinks that Mohsin's pen-name, "Fani", means "Perishable". So much for the author and title. Its use? Well, according to the Introduction in the American edition by Professor A. V. Williams Jackson of Columbia University, it is "a work by an Oriental and written for Orientals, but we of the West may equally profit by its contents".

But "Fani" does not mean perishable; when used as a pen-name it more accurately signifies *Transient*; and it is the kind of name taken by Sufis or Sufi-minded people to refer to the passing through this world which Sufis feel to be a halting place. And Fani, according to report, was a follower of the Sufis, and an associate of Prince Dara Shikoh, the Indian Sufi of the Moghul imperial family. And "School of Manners" is not the meaning of

"Dabistán". The word stands for *The Abode of Pomp, Ostentation*, and the book's title refers to the outward appearance of religion as catalogued in the twelve faiths dealt with within its covers. And its meaning to people of the West, three hundred years after its composition and nearly a hundred and forty years after its first English publication? Certainly to add to the immense contemporary documentation of Sufism and to show what people of those times (the Mughal and later the British) thought of Sufism and the Sufis.

The author himself summarises the contents of the work in this way:

> "In this book, called 'The Dabistán', is contained something of the knowledge and faith of past nations, of the speeches and actions of modern people, as it has been reported by those who know what is manifest, and see what is concealed; as well as by those who are attached to exterior forms, and by those who discern the inward meaning, without omission, and diminution, without hatred, envy and scorn, and without taking a part for the one, or against the other side of the question".

The *Dabistán* deals with twelve religions, including Christianity, Islam, Judaism and various cults and schools. The forms of belief are identified as religions in the Sufi manner of regarding as a religion the beliefs by which people live or are seen to live: not necessarily assuming that a people's religion is what they say it is. In this respect, of course, the Sufi attitude comes close to the modern diagnosis of belief-systems. Hence someone calling himself a Christian who did not obey its tenets would not be regarded as one — and someone who (for example) imagined that he had no religion but relied on astrology or mascots would be of that "religion".

This present version is confined to the section of the *Dabistán* devoted to the Sufis, and is the concluding part of the book.

Quite a number of statements and quotations in this work illustrate the oddly modern perception of human behaviour (looked at from the Western standpoint) which marks much Sufi commentary. We note, for example, that pious show, the display of religion, is seen as a form of vanity and self-indulgence. Further even private performance of religious rituals was clearly noted in those supposedly ignorant times as being a possible barrier to higher understanding and real spirituality, when they are only used for emotion stimulus. There is a lesson here for the many millions who are exposed to present-day cults which offer excitement and a sense of significance without making sure that their followers have first done something about their vanity.

PRELIMINARY DISCOURSE

How the Dabistan first became known — its author — the sources of his information

It is generally known that Sir William Jones was the first who drew the attention of Orientalists to the Dabistán. This happened five years after the beginning of a new era in Oriental literature, the foundation of the Asiatic Society of Calcutta by that illustrious man. It may not appear inopportune here to revive the grateful remembrance of one who acquired the uncontested merit of not only exciting in Asia and Europe a new ardor for Oriental studies, but also of directing them to their great objects — MAN and NATURE; and of endeavoring, by word and deed, to render the attainment of languages conducive to the required knowledge equally easy and attractive.

Having, very early in life, gained a European reputation as a scholar and elegant writer, Sir William Jones embarked[1] for the Indian shores with vast projects, embracing, with the extension of science, the general improvement of mankind.[2] Four months after his arrival

[1] In April, 1783.
[2] He landed at Calcutta in September, 1783.

in Calcutta,[1] he addressed as the first president of the Asiatic Society, a small but select assembly, in which he found minds responsive to his own noble sentiments. A rapid sketch of the first labors of their incomparable leader, may not be irrelevant to our immediate subject.

In his second anniversary discourse,[2] he proposed a general plan for investigating Asiatic learning, history, and institutions. In his third discourse, he traced the line of investigation, which he faithfully followed, as long as he lived in India, in his annual public speeches: he determined to exhibit the prominent features of the five principal nations of Asia — the Indians, Arabs, Tartars, Persians, and Chinese. After having treated in the two following years of the Arabs and Tartars, he considered in his sixth discourse[3] the Persians, and declared that he had been induced by his earliest investigations to believe, and by his latest to conclude, that three primitive races of men must have migrated originally from a central country, and that this country was *Iran*, commonly called Persia. Examining with particular care the traces of the most ancient languages and religions which had prevailed in this country, he rejoiced at "a fortunate discovery, for which", he said, "he was first indebted to Mir Muhammed Hussain, one of the most intelligent Muselmans in India, and which has at once dissipated the cloud, and cast a gleam of light on the primeval history of Iran and of the human race, of which he had long despaired, and which could hardly have dawned from any other quarter;" this was, he declared, "the rare and interesting tract on twelve different religions, entitled the DABISTÁN".[4]

Sir William Jones read the Dabistán for the first time in 1787. I cannot refrain from subjoining here the opinion upon this work, which he communicated in a

[1] In January, 1784.
[2] Delivered in February, 1785.
[3] In February, 1789.
[4] The Works of Sir William Jones, with the life of the author, by Lord Teignmouth, in 13 vols. Vol. III, p. 110. 1807.

private letter, dated June, 1787, to J. Shore, Esq. (afterwards Lord Teignmouth); he says: "The greatest part of it would be very interesting to a curious reader, but some of it cannot be translated. It contains more recondite learning, more entertaining history, more beautiful specimens of poetry, more ingenuity and wit, more indecency and blasphemy, than I ever saw collected in a single volume;[1] the two last are not of the author's, but are introduced in the chapters on the heretics and infidels of India.[2] On the whole, it is the most amusing and instructive book I ever read in Persian".[3]

We may suppose it was upon the recommendation of Sir William Jones, that Francis Gladwin, one of the most distinguished members of the new Society, translated the first chapter of *The Dabistán*, or "School of Manners", which title has been preserved from due regard to the meritorious Orientalist, who first published the translation of a part of this work. The whole of it was printed in the year 1809, in Calcutta, and translations of some parts of it were published in *The Asiatic Researches*.[4] It is only at present, more than half a century after the first public notice of it by Sir W. Jones, that the version of the whole work appears, under the auspices and at the expense of the Oriental Translation Committee of Great Britain and Ireland.

Who was the author of the Dabistán? — Sir William Jones thought it was composed by a Muhammedan traveller, a native of Kachmir, named *Mohsan*, but dis-

---

[1] I shall hereafter give some explanations upon this subject.

[2] There appears in the printed edition no positive ground for the opinion above expressed; we find, however, frequent repetitions of the same subject, such as are not likely to belong to the same author; we know, besides, that additions and interpolations are but too common in all Oriental manuscripts.

[3] The Persian text, with the translation of the first chapter, appeared in the two first numbers of the *New Asiatic Miscellany*, Calcutta, 1789. This English version was rendered into German by Dalberg, 1809.

[4] These translations are mentioned in the notes of the present version.

tinguished by the assumed surname of *Fání*, "the Perishable".

Gladwin[1] calls him *Shaikh Muhammed Mohsin*, and says that, besides the Dabistán, he has left behind him a collection of poems, among which there is a moral essay, entitled *Masdur ul asas*, "the source of signs"; he was of the philosophic sect of Súfis, and patronised by the imperial prince *Dara Shikoh*, whom he survived; among his disciples in philosophy is reckoned *Muhammed Tahir*, surnamed *Ghawri*, whose poems are much admired in Hindostan. Mohsan's death is placed in the year of the Hejira 1081 (A.D. 1670).

William Erskine,[2] in search of the true author of the Dabistán, discovered no other account of Mohsan Fání than that contained in the *Gul-i-Râana*, "charming rose", of *Lachmi Narayán*, who flourished in Hyderabad about the end of the 18th or the beginning of the 19th century. This author informs us, under the article of Mohsan Fání, that "Mohsán, a native of Kachmir, was a learned man and a respectable poet; a scholar of *Mulla Yakub*, Súfi of Kachmir; and that, after completing his studies, he repaired to Delhi, to the court of the emperor *Shah Jehan*, by whom, in consequence of his great reputation and high acquirements, he was appointed *Sadder*, 'chief judge', of Allahabad; that there he became a disciple of Shaikh *Mohib ulla*, an eminent doctor of that city, who wrote the treatise entitled *Teswich*, 'the golden Mean'. Mohsan Fání enjoyed this honorable office till Shah Jehân subdued Balkh; at which time *Nazer Muhammed Khan*, the Wali, 'prince', of Balkh, having effected his escape, all his property was plundered. It happened that in his library there was found a copy of Mohsan's Diwán, or 'poetical Collection', which contained an ode in praise of the (fugitive) Wáli. This gave such offence to the emperor, that the Sadder was disgraced and lost his office, but was generously allowed a pension. He retired (as Lachmi informs us) to his native country, where he

---

[1] New Asiatic Misc., p. 87.
[2] Transactions of the Literary Society of Bombay, vol. II, p. 374.

passed the rest of his days without any public employment, happy and respected. His house was frequented by the most distinguished men of Kachmir, and among the rest by the governors of the province. He had lectures at his house, being accustomed to read to his audience the writings of certain authors of eminence, on which he delivered moral and philosophical comments. Several scholars of note, among whom were Taher Ghawri (before mentioned) and *Haji Aslem Salem*, issued from his school. He died on the before mentioned date. It is to be observed that Lachmi does not mention the Dabistán as a production of Mohsan Fání, though, had he written it, it must have been his most remarkable work".

Erskine goes on to recapitulate some particulars mentioned in the Dabistán of the author's life, and concludes that it seems very improbable that Mohsan Fání and the author of the Dabistán were the same person. In this conclusion, and upon the same grounds, he coincides with the learned Vans Kennedy.[1]

Erskine further quotes,[2] from a manuscript copy of the Dabistán which he saw in the possession of Mulla Firuz, in Bombay, the following marginal note annexed to the close of chapter XIV: "In the city of Daurse, a king of the Parsis, of the race of the imperial Anushirván, The Shet Dawer Huryár, conversed with *Amír Zulfikar Ali-al-Husaini* (on whom be the grace of God!), whose poetical name was Mobed Shah". This Zulfikar Ali, whoever he was, the Mulla supposes to be the author of the Dabistán. Erskine judiciously subjoins: "On so slight an authority, I would not willingly set up an unknown author as the compiler of that work; but it is to be remarked that many verses of Mobed's are quoted in the Dabistán, and there is certainly reason to suspect that the poetical Mobed, whoever he may be, was the author of that compilation".

"To this let it be added, that the author of the

---

[1] Transactions of the Literary Society of Bombay, vol. II, pp. 243–244.
[2] Ibid., pp. 375–376.

Dabistán, in his account of Mobed Serosh, says[1] that one Muhammed Mohsan, a man of learning, told him that he had heard Mobed Serosh give three hundred and sixty proofs of the existence of God. This at least makes Muhammed Mohsan, whoever he may be, a different person from the author of the Dabistán".

I cannot omit adding the following notice annexed to the note quoted above: "Between the printed copy and Mulla Firuz's manuscript before alluded to, a difference occurs in the very beginning of the work. After the poetical address to the Deity and the praise of the prophet, with which the Dabistán, like most other Muselman works, commences, the manuscript reads: 'Mohsan Fani says', and two moral couplets succeed. In the printed copy, the words 'Mohsan Fani says', — which should occur between the last word of the first page and the first word of the second — are omitted. As no account of the author is given in the beginning of the book, as is usual with Muselman writers, Mulla Firuz conjectures that a careless or ignorant reader may have considered the words 'Mohsan Fáni says' as forming the commencement of the volume, and as containing the name of the author of the whole book; whereas they merely indicate the author of the couplets that follow, and would rather show that Mohsan Fani was not the writer of the Dabistán. This conjecture, I confess, appears to me at once extremely ingenious and very probable. A comparison of different manuscripts might throw more light on the question".

Concerning the opinion last stated, I can but remark, that in a manuscript copy of the Dabistán, which I procured from the library of the King of Oude, and caused to be transcribed for me, the very same words: "Mohsan Fani says", occur (as I have observed in vol. I, p. 6, note 3), preceding a *rabaâ*, or quatrain, which begins:

---

[1] See the present Transl., vol. I, pp. 113–114. A mistake is here to be pointed out: at p. 114, I. ii, the name of Kaivan has been substituted for that of Mobed Serosh.

"The world is a book full of knowledge and of justice", etc. etc.

These lines seem well chosen as an introduction to the text itself, which begins by a summary of the whole work, exhibiting the titles of the twelve chapters of which it is composed. As the two copies mentioned (the one found in Bombay, the other in Lucknow) contain the same words, they can hardly be taken for an accidental addition of a copyist. I found no remark upon this point in Mr. Shea's translation, who had two manuscript copies to refer to. Whatever it be, it must still remain undecided, whether Mohsan Fani was there named only as the author of the next quatrain or of the whole book, although either hypothesis may not appear destitute of probability; nor can it be considered strange to admit that the name of Mohsan Fani was borne by more than one individual. I shall be permitted to continue calling the author of the Dabistán by the presumed name of Mohsan Fani.

Dropping this point, we shall now search for information upon his person, character, and knowledge in the work itself. Is he really a native of Kachmir, as here before stated?

Although in the course of his book he makes frequent mention of Kachmir, he never owns himself a native of that country. In one part of his narrative, he expressly alludes to another home. He begins the second chapter upon the religion of the Hindus (vol. II, p. 2) by these words: "As inconstant fortune had torn away the author from the shores of Persia, and made him the associate of the believers in transmigration and those who addressed their prayers to idols and images, and worshipped demons..." Now we know that Kachmir is considered as a very ancient seat, nay as the very cradle, of the doctrine of transmigration, and of Hinduism in general, with all its tenets, rites, and customs; and that from the remotest times to the present it was inhabited by numerous adherents of this faith; how could the author, if a native of Kachmir, accuse inconstant fortune for having made him elsewhere an associate of these very religionists with whom, from his birth, he must have been accustomed to live? The passage just quoted leaves scarce a doubt that the shores of Persia, from which he bewails having been torn, were really his native country.

When was he born?

He nowhere adduces the date of his birth; the earliest period of his life which he mentions, is the year of the Hejira 1028 (A.D. 1618):[1] in this year the Mobed Hushíar brought the author to Balik Nátha, a great adept in the Yoga, or ascetic devotion, to receive the blessing of that holy man, who pronounced these words over him: "This boy shall acquire the knowledge of God". It is not stated in what place this happened. The next earliest date is five years later, 1033 of the Hejira (A.D. 1623).[2] He says that, in his infancy, he came with his friends and relations from Patna to the capital Akbarabad, and was carried in the arms of the Mobed Hushíar to Chatur Vapah, a famous ascetic of those days. The pious man rejoiced at it, and bestowed his blessing on the future writer of the Dabistán; he taught him the *mantra*, "prayer", of the sun, and appointed one of his disciples to remain with the boy until the age of manhood. We have here a positive statement: in the year 1623 A.D., he was "in his infancy", and carried "in the arms of his protector". Giving the widest extension to these expressions, we can hardly think him to have been either much older or younger than seven or eight years: not much older, for being in some way carried in the arms of the Mobed; nor much younger, having been taught a hymn to the sun, and he might have been a boy of three years when he received the first-mentioned blessing from Balik Natha. We may therefore suppose him to have been born about the year 1615 of our era, in the tenth year of the reign of the emperor Jehangir. We collect in his work fifty-three dates relative to himself between the year 1618 and 1653. From 1627 to 1643, we see him mostly in Kachmir and Lahore, travelling between these two

---

[1] See vol. II, p. 137.
[2] See vol. II. p. 145.

places; in 1643, he was at the holy sepulchre, probably at Meshhad, which appears to be the furthermost town to the West which he reached; from 1634 to 1649, he dwelt in several towns of the Panjab and Guzerat; the next year he proceeded to Sikakul, the remotest town in the East which he says he has visited; there he fell sick, and sojourned during 1653, at which epoch, if the year of his birth be correctly inferred, he had attained his thirty-eighth year. We have no other date of his death than that before stated: if he died in 1670, it was in the eleventh year of the reign of Aurengzéb, or Alemgir. Mohsan Fani would therefore have passed his infancy, youth, and manhood mostly in India, under the reigns of the three emperors, Jehangír, Shah Jehan, and Aurengzeb.[1] It was the state of religion, prevailing in those days in Hindostan that he describes.

From his earliest age he appears to have led an active life, frequently changing his residence. Such a mode of life belongs to a travelling merchant or philosopher, and in our author both qualities might have been united, as is often the case in Asia. Mohsan Fani, during his travels, collected the diversified and curious materials for the Dabistán; he observed with his own eyes the manners and customs of different nations and sects. He says himself at the conclusion of his work: "After having much frequented the meetings of the followers of the five before-said religions", Magians, Hindus, Jews, Nazareans, and Muselmans, "the author wished and undertook to write this book; and whatever in this work, treating of the religions of different countries, is stated concerning the creed of different sects, has been taken from their books, and for the account of the persons belonging to any particular sect, the author's information was imparted to him by their adherents and sincere friends, and recorded literally, so that no trace of partiality nor aversion might be perceived: in short, the writer of these pages performed no more than the task of

---

[1] Jehangir reigned from 1605 to 1628. Shah Jehan from 1628 to 1659. Aurengzeb from 1659 to 1707.

a translator". This declaration, even to a severe critic, may appear satisfactory. Sir William Jones called him[1] a learned and accurate, a candid and ingenious author. A further appreciation of Mohsan Fani's character is reserved for subsequent pages. We can, however, here state, that he sought the best means of information, and gives us what he had acquired not only from personal experience, which is always more or less confined; not only from oral instruction, which is too often imperfectly given and received; but also from an attentive perusal of the best works which he could procure upon the subject of his investigation. Of the latter authorities which the author produces, some are known in Europe, and we may judge of the degree of accuracy and intelligence with which he has made use of them. Of others, nothing at all, or merely the name, is known. . . . .

THE RELIGION OF THE SUFIS

We arrive at the last chapter, "*Upon the Sufis*"; the most abstruse of the twelve, but to which we are well enough prepared by the contents of the former.

Súfism, according to the Dabistán, belongs to all religions; its adherents are known, under different names among the Hindus, Persians, and Arabians; it appears to be nothing else but the rationalism of any sort of doctrine. It could never be the religion of a whole nation; it remained confined to the precincts of schools and societies.

In the work before us we find it stated, that the belief of the pure Súfis was the same as that of the Ashrakians (Platonists): we know what the Muhammedans have made of it. According to the Imám Koshairi, quoted by Jâmi,[2] the Muselmans, after Muhammed's death, distinguished the eminent men among them by no other title but that of "the companions of God's apostle". These were, in the second generation, called *Tábáyún*,

---

[1] The Works of Sir W. Jones, vol. IV, pp. 16 and 105.

[2] See *Journal des Savans, décembre* 1821, pp. 721, 722, *art. de Silvestre de Sacy.*

"followers". Afterwards the Islamites were divided into divers classes; those among them who particularly devoted themselves to the practice of religion, were named "servants of God", which name was, after the rise of numerous sects, claimed by some from among all the different sectaries. It was then that the followers of the orthodox doctrine, in order to preserve the purity of their faith and the strength of their piety, assumed the name of *Súfis*, which name became celebrated before the end of the second century of the Hejira, that is, before the year 815 of our era. We may believe one of the greatest scholars of Muhammedism, *Ghazáli*, who ranged himself among the Súfis of his time towards the end of our eleventh century, when he declares that in their society he found rest in believing one God, the prophet, and the last judgment: this is the faith of the *orthodox Súfis*.

The assumption of any particular name carries men, who so distinguish and separate themselves from their fellows, much further than they themselves at first intended, particularly when the distinction and separation are founded upon vague and indeterminate notions of metaphysics. Under the impression, that there are secrets upon which their salvation depends, they will stretch reason and imagination to penetrate them. The Súfis are divided, according to their own phraseology,[1] into three classes: "*the attracted, the travellers,* and *the attracted travellers*"; the last of whom combine the qualities of the two former. I will class them here, with respect to their doctrine and manners, into five orders.

1. The religious Súfis, in general, are occupied with something beyond the limits of our natural consciousness; they exercise to the utmost their inward organ or inner sense, and acquire a philosophic imagination —

"The vision and the faculty divine".[2]

[1] The *Sa'lik, Mejezub,* and *Mejezub Salik.* (See A Treatise on Sufism, or Muhammedan Mysticism, by Lieutenant J. William Graham. In the Transact. of the Lit. Soc. of Bombay, vol. I, p. 99, 1811.)

[2] Wordsworth.

Such was the prophetic gift of Muhammed, and as long as they adhere to his sayings, they are the *orthodox Súfis*, whom I have already mentioned.

2. Another order endeavor to comprehend, to fix, and to explain the attributes of God; the holy object sanctifies their efforts; unattainable, it exalts their souls above themselves; incomprehensibility yields to the sacred power of self-intuition; mysterious darkness to celestial light; their intellect, no more terrestrial, "knows its own sun and its own stars";[1] by continual mental excitement they produce in themselves (according to their own phraseology) a state of intoxication; in the full enjoyment of their liberty, they approach the Supreme Being, and finally fancy an intimate union with their Creator. These are the *mystic Sufis*.

Man, to express his most fervent adoration of the Divinity, uses the expressions by which he is wont to address the object of his most tender affections; he has but the fire of earth to kindle in sacrifice to heaven; and to elevate his soul to the Supreme Being, he makes wings of the most lively sentiments which he ever experienced, and can excite in himself. The intensity of inward feeling breaks loose in outward demonstrations, gesture, song, and dance —

"Mystical dance, which yonder starry sphere
Of planets, and of fix'd, in all her wheels
Resembles nearest, mazes intricate,
Eccentric, intervolv'd, yet regular,
Then most, when most irregular they seem".[2]

Such in the poet's eye is the dance of angels, but less refined must be that of mortals, and really one sort of it strangely contrasts with the usually grave deportment of bearded ample-robed Muselmans, from Muhammed, who gave the example, down to the Durvishes of our days, who, with frantic howls and vehement whirling motions, by ludicrous and unseemly exhibition, destroy the whole gravity of inward intention. Mohsan Fani

---

[1] "――― Solemque suum, sua sidera norunt."
Aeneis, c. VI. v. 641.

[2] Milton's Paradise Lost, V., v. 620–624.

adduces some instances of dancing, and quotes throughout his work verses of mystical poetry upon Divine love, in glowing expressions belonging to profane passion. It is known how equivocal in their meaning they appear in the works of Jelal eddin Rumi, Sâdi, Hafiz, and others.[1]

3. It was not always vehement enthusiasm which was nourished in the contemplation of one Supreme Being; mysticism, in Súfis of a milder character, became *quietism: he to whom all things are one, who draweth all things to one, and seeth all things in one, may enjoy peace and rest of spirit.* I have quoted the words of an English bishop, Jeremy Taylor, and might borrow similar passages from a more ancient Christian bishop, Synesius,[2] for expressing a sort of purely *spiritual pantheism.* But there is another, which seems not to exclude materialism: the great cause from which the infinite series of all material and spiritual existences originates, is enveloped, as it were, with the vest of the universe; never known as to its essence, but always felt in its manifestations; it is

"All in all, and all in every part".[3]

In short, God is all, and all is God. This appeared not more incomprehensible, but less complicated than any other system to the *pantheistical Súfis.*

4. After excessive efforts to transcend the limits of his nature, the philosophic inquirer re-enters into himself, and coerces his futile attempts by the precept: "Know thyself". Having, as it were, recovered himself, and feeling that every thing proceeds from the depth of his mind, he sees himself in every thing; heaven and earth are his own; "he demands from himself whatever he wishes"; for he is every thing; he finds the God whom he sought in himself, in his own heart, and says, "Who

---

[1] The two first give their name to the mystic and moral age; from 1203 to 1300; the third to that of the highest splendor of Persian lyrical poetry and rhetoric, from 1300 to 1397 of our era. — (See *Schöne Redekünste Persiens Von Joseph Von Hammer, Wien,* 1818.)

[2] He was born in Cyrene, in Africa, towards the end of our fourth century, and died, about 430, bishop of Ptolemais.

[3] Cowley.

knows himself, knows God". This is religious psychology, the creed of the *egotist class of Súfis*.

It is a fact which appears incredible, but is too well attested for the admission of a doubt, that Súfis believed themselves to be gods, and adhered to their belief, amid torments, until death.[1] This psychological fact may be explained by considering that, according to Súfism, God is nothing else but an idea of the highest perfection; *he*, says our author, *from whose sight both worlds vanished, who in the steps of right faith arrived at the rank of perfect purity, from truth to truth, became God*; that is, he became one with his own idea of perfection, which cannot be disputed to him; his divinity is an illusion, but nothing else to him is the world; it is all and nothing, dependent upon his own creation and annihilation.

5. Transacting as it were directly with the Divine Being, the Súfis throw off the shackles of the positive religion; pious rebels, they neither fast nor make pilgrimages to the temple of Mecca, nay, they forget their prayers; for with God there is no other but the soundless language of the heart. From excess of religion they have no religion at all. Thus is confirmed the trite saying that "extremes meet". "*The perfection of a man's state*", says Jami, "*and the utmost degree to which saints may attain, is to be without an attribute, and without a mark*". The most fervent zeal sinks into the coldest indifference about religion. The author of the Dabistán declares positively, that "whoever says that the Muselmans are above the Christians, does not know the true Being". But the whole creed of an *emancipated* (this is the name I give to one belonging to the fifth order of Súfis) uniting in himself the egotist, pantheistic, and mystical Súfi will be found in the following verses of Jelal-eddin Rúmi, before mentioned:[2]

"O Moslims! what is to be done? I do not myself; I am neither Jew, nor Christian, nor Gueber, nor Moslim; I am not from the East nor from the West; nor from land nor sea;

[1] See p. 74 n. 1.
[2] I follow the German translation of Baron von Hammer, *loc. cit.*, p. 189.

neither from the region of nature nor from that of heaven; not from Hind nor China; not from Bulgaria nor Irak, nor from the towns of Khorassan. I am neither water nor dust, wind nor fire; not from the highest nor deepest, neither self-existent nor created; I am not from the two worlds, no son of Adam, not from hell nor from heaven, nor paradise. He is the first, the last, the interior, the exterior; I know but him, Yahu! Yahu! Menhu! I looked up, and saw both worlds to be one; I see but one – I seek but one – I know but one. My station is without space, my mark without impression, it is not soul nor body; I am the soul of souls. If I had passed one single day without thee, I would repent to have lived one single hour. When one day the friend stretches out his hand to me in solitude, I tread the worlds under my feet, and open my hands. O Shams Tabrizi,[1] I am so intoxicated here that, except intoxication, no other remedy remains to me."

We know, by the preceding, what the Súfi is not; we shall now learn what he is.[2]

"O Moslims! I am intoxicated by love in the world. I am a believer – an unbeliever – a drunken monk; I am the Shaikhs Bayazid, Shubli, Juneid, Abu Hanifa, Shafei, Hanbeli; I the throne and tent of heaven, from the dust up to the Pleyads; I am whatever thou seest in separation and enjoyment; I am the distance of two bows-length[3] around the throne; I am the Gospel, the Psalter, the Koran; I am *Usa* and *Lat*,[4] the cross, the *Bál* and *Dagon*,[5] the Kâbah, and the place of sacrifice. The world is divided into seventy-and-two sects, but there is but one God; the believer in him and I; I am the lie, the truth, the good, the evil, the hard and the soft, science, solitude, virtue, faith, the deepest pit of hell,

---

[1] Shams-eddin Tabrisi, whom Jelal-eddin names at the end of nearly all his lyric poems, is said to have been the son of Khuand Ala-eddin, chief of the Assassins (Ismàilahs). He gained a great celebrity as a Súfi and a saint. From Tabriz, from which town he took his surname, he came to Konia; there Jelal-eddin chose him for his spiritual guide, and remained attached to him all his life, which terminated A.D. 1262. Shams-eddin survived him. The tombs of the master and disciple, near each other in Konia, are even in our days objects of veneration to pious Muselmans.

[2] *Ibid.*, p. 191.

[3] The distance to which Muhammed approached God in heaven.

[4] Two Arabian idols, the Dusares and Allitta of Herodotus.

[5] Syrian deities.

the greatest torment of flames, the highest paradise, Huti, Risvan,¹ am I. What is the intent of his speech? Say it, O Shams Tabrizi! The intended meaning is: I am the soul of the world".

After having sounded human nature in its depth, and viewed it in its various forms, the Muhammedan philosophers conceived a high idea of man in general, and call him *insan kamil,* "the perfect man". He is the reunion of all the worlds, divine and natural, universal and partial; he is the book, the pure, sublime, and venerable pages of which are not to be touched, nor can be comprehended, but by those who have thrown off the dark veils of ignorance. His soul is to his body what the universal soul is to the great world, which bears the name of "the great man".

Sir William Jones refers,[2] for a particular detail of Súfi metaphysics and theology, to the Dabistán. These are given with a particular phraseology, for which it is not easy to find corresponding expressions in any European language; and which I have endeavored, to the best of my power, to explain in my notes. A particular signification is attached even to the most common terms, such as state, station, time, duration, existence, non-existence, possibility, presence, absence, testimony, sanctity, annihilation, etc., etc. Besides, we find particular divisions and classifications: different attributions and names of the Deity, the unity of which is to be preserved in all; the division of spirits, prophetism, true and false miracles, revelation, inspiration; four sorts of mankind, as many of life and death; seven degrees of contemplative life, in each of which degrees the Súfi sees a different color; four lights of God; four sorts of manifestations, the sign of which is annihilation, called "the science", or "positive knowledge". Further we meet with a metempsychosis for the imperfect soul, and an *appearance* for the perfect; even with a geography of the invisible, the land

[1] The guardian of paradise.

[2] In his Treatise on the mystical poetry of the Persians and Hindus: vol. IV of his Works, p. 232.

of shades in the towns of *Jabilkha, Jabilsa* and *Barzah*, etc., etc.; and, in addition, manifold opinions of Asiatic philosophy.

Here should be pointed out how Muhammedan or other Súfis may be confounded with the Hindu Yogis or Sanyásis, although in reality distinguishable from each other. The Yajur Veda, and other sacred books of the latter inculcate the precept that a man ought to acquire perfect indifference concerning the whole exterior world, and in all places to lay aside the notion of diversity. This is what a Yogi or Sanyasi endeavors to attain: he quits every thing, house, wife, children, even his *caste*; the world has no more right upon him than he upon the world. In this he agrees with the Súfi; but the latter generally aspires to the divine gift of inspiration, prophetism, mystical enthusiasm, whilst the common state of a Yogi is that of complete impassiveness or torpor.

It is only towards the end of the Dabistán that Mohsan Fani mentions particularly the *Sabeans*, whose religion was, from the very beginning of the work, treated of under different names of the ancient Persian religions, such as *Yezdanians, Jamsaspians*, etc., etc.

THE RELIGION OF THE SUFIS

Of the Religion of the Sufiahs,[1] contained in three Sections

Section I. — Some of their tenets.
Section II. — The open interpretation of their open confessions.
Section III. — Some individuals among them.

Section I. — Of some of their tenets

These sectaries, like other philosophers, always were, and are, scattered among all nations of the world, and

---

[1] Several derivations are given to the word *Sufí*; it may be here sufficient to adduce the three most specious of them. Some derive the name from the verb صفا , *Sa fá*, "he was sincere, pure"; this derivation is claimed by these sectaries themselves, who frequently call themselves اصفيا , *Asfíá*, "pure", as may be seen in Jami's work, *Tohfat ol ebrar*, "a present offered to the pious": and in *Gulshenraz* (work quoted). To this etymology is objected, that a substantive derived from the said verb should be صفى , and not صوفى . Others deduce it with grammatical strictness from صوف *súf*, "wool", and *sufí* signifies therefore "wool-dressed". But the fact is, that not all wool-dressed persons are Súfis, and not all Súfis are wool-dressed: a Súfi may wear a Durvish's patched coat, or satin; as it was said by a true Súfi. If, of the two etymologies quoted, the first does not answer the grammatical construction, the second does not render the meaning to be expressed. The latter appears to me so much more important, that I am disposed to pass over an anomalous construction, which in other names is not without numerous examples. Nor would I be averse to derive the word, with other etymologists, from the Greek σοφος , "wise", or σαφες , "pure"; notwithstanding the general use of representing in words of Greek derivation the *sigma*, Σ , by a *sin*, س , and not by a *sad*, ص , if I did not perceive a great difference between the doctrine of a *Sofos* and that of a *Súfi*, which latter bears most especially an Asiatic character, and the origin of which remounts to the kings Mahabad and Jemshid (*Dasátir*, Eng. Transl., pp. 23, 97). Our author says: "Súfism is to be found among all nations". The first Muhammedan Súfi is said to have

are called in Persian *vèzhahderún*, "internally pure", or *róuchen-dil*, "enlightened minds", or *Yèkána-bín*, "seers of unity"; in the Hindu language, *Rakhísher* (Rakshasas) and *Tapísher* (Tapasis) *Gyanisher* and *Gyáni* (Jnánis), or *Atma-jnánis*. The lord *Maulavi Jámi*, in his work entitled *Resálah-i-vajudíah*, "treatise upon existence",[1] states, that the universal Being is distinct from any intellectual and exterior existence, inasmuch as every individual from among the intellectual and exterior beings belongs to some class of beings; but the universal Being is not subordinate to the condition of any thing; he is absolute and sovereign, and not general, not partial, not special, not common, and not one by (the number of) unity; for, it is neither a substance nor an accident, but by itself one, and not a multiple. These things however are necessary in the sovereign being, according to their degrees and stations,[2] but the real Being, under the condition of no substance whatever, is distinguished by the name *martibah-ahadiyat*,[3] "degree of unity", and all names and attributes are (as it were) consumed by this degree, which the Yogis express by the title *hakiket al hakáyek*,[4] "reality of realities". But the real Being, under the condition of all things which are necessarily himself, according to generalities and specialities, is called by names and attributes of the divine degree, and this degree is entitled *Vahedet-i-mokam*,[5] "solitariness of station", and *jamah*,[6]

been *Abu Hashem*, a native of Kufa, who died in the year of the Hejira 150 (A.D. 767). — (See *Notices et Extraits des manuscrits de la bibliothèque du Roi et d'autres bibliothèques*, vol. X, p. 290.) The origin of such a character among Muselmans, if not in name, yet in fact, may be traced further back to the first century of the Hejira.

[1] The more correct title of this work is *Resalah fil vujud*. — (See *Geschichte der Schönen Redekünste Persiens von Joseph von Hammer*, S. 314.)

[2] .بحسب مراتب و مقامات

[3] .مرتبه احديت

[4] .حقيقت الحقايق

[5] .وحدت مقام

[6] .جمع

"union". The real Being, under no condition of "a thing" (*shí*),¹ and under no condition of "nothing" (*láshí*),² is called *húvíyat*,³ "essence, absolute being, objectivity", and it is manifesting itself⁴ in all existences, and under the condition of "a thing and nothing", is the form of the universe.⁵

Some of the sagacious have stated that, in the same manner as the sun is radiant, so the real Being manifests himself at once; for in opposition to it is *âdem*, "non-entity", and from the superabundance of manifestation the tongue and language (in the effort) to express and to describe, to define and to explain, become dumb. The final explanation of the two words, *vojud*, "existence", and *âdem*, "non-entity" may be, that existence is the negation of non-entity, and non-entity the negation of existence; and the Lord of unity is the grand origin of the multiplicity of names and attributes. The first attribute, which emerged into manifestation by this Lord from within, was intelligence; and in this degree all *aâyán sabitah*, "fixed realities",⁶ were under intellectual forms, and in this degree the Súfis give to the true highest and absolute Being the name of "All-Wise". The impulsion of divine wisdom to procure to his fixed ideals the

¹ شَیْ.
² لَاشَیْ.

³ هُوِیَت, a substantive formed from هُو, *hu*, "he is" (*Yahu Yehovah*).

⁴ I interpret in this place the word *sárí* in the sense which is given to it by the commentator of the Gulshen Raz, in a passage of that work which will be quoted hereafter.

⁵ The above *shí* and *láshí* is evidently the *sad asat*, "being, not being", of the Hindus, an attribute of the divinity, combined with its unity. "For", says the author of Gulshen Raz (see German Transl., p. 17), "unity exists in non-existence as well as in existence; multiplicity proceeds but from relation; difference and variety of things proceed from the change of the possible: as the existence of both is but one, they furnish the proof that God is but one".

⁶ اعیان الثابته. *Aâyan* signifies "substances": these are things which maintain themselves by themselves; or realities, which occupy a space by themselves, without their existence in space depending upon the concomitant existence of another thing. This is the

superiority over non-entity is by them entitled *irâdet*,[1] "providence", and the name of *murid*, "he who wills", attached to God. As often as the divine knowledge becomes joined to accomplishment and victory, as having given to the existence of knowledge the superiority over contingencies, in this degree they call this victory *kadaret*, "might"; and in this degree originated the name of *Kadir*, "Almighty". With respect to the seeing of God, as the meaning of knowledge is his presence in face of the existing external figures of contingencies, in this degree, the name of *Bâsír*, "the All-Seeing", offered itself. Likewise, the meditation upon God, by those who, praying, recite his emblematic

contrary of accidents, the existence of which depends upon the concomitant existence of the substance which serves to support them, or which is the place by which they are supported. *Aâyân sabitah*, that is, "fixed substances", are realities of things inclosed in the science of God, that is to say, the figures of realities of divine names in the *scientific presence*. They are posterior to God only as to essence, and not as to time; for they are eternal, as much on the side of the past as on the side of the future. When it is said, that God produces them by emanation, the posteriority which is thereby expressed, refers but to essence, and is not true in any other sense. — (See *Jorjani's Definitions in Ext. et Not. des MSS.*, vol. X, p. 65.) — We may, in a language more familiar to us perhaps, express them by "eternal ideals", or "prototypes of realities". Silvestre de Sacy adds to Jorjani's explanation, that the question is here about divine names, that is, attributes of God as emanating from his essence, and residing in him, but not yet produced externally by any action. The *scientific presence* mentioned in this explanation appears, to him, to signify the divine majesty, inasmuch as manifesting its presence to beings which have no other existence but in the science of God.

[1] ارادت , "inclination, design, will", According to *Jorjáni's Definitions* (see *Ext. et Not. des MSS.*, vol. X, p. 37), *iradet* is a quality which produces in a living being a state, the effect of which is that he acts in one manner rather than in another. In its exact sense, it is a faculty which has no other object in view but that which does not exist; for "the will" is an attribute, the special object of which is to give existence to any thing, and to produce it conformably with the words of the Koran: "*When he wills a thing he says to it: "Be", and it is*". *Iradet* is also interpreted an inclination to any thing which follows the opinion of utility, and in this sense I have translated it above "providence".

attributes, is the time of propitiating; and the granting of these prayers is called *samíâ*, "hearing": whence proceeded the name samíâ, "hearer". Further, the will of God, the Highest, becoming concentrated in this state, having joined the letter *kaf* (k) to the letter *nún* (n), so as to manifest by action *kun faíkun*,[1] "Be, and it is": this state they called *kalám*, "the word", and the name of *mutkalem*, "speaker", was produced on this account.

The lord Shaikh Muhammed Shosterí,[2] in his treatise *Hak al yakín*,[3] "the truth of conviction", has stated, that the action of choice prevails with the self-existent Being over necessity, because choice is presupposed in the nature of might, and provident choice, as well as vicissitudes and excitement, are parts suitable to a purpose, and providence came to succour every one of the necessitous crowd, by procreating remedies against the evils without number which are determined by necessity, in opposition to that necessity whence pure procreation proceeds. When the free agent is straitened in his choice, then choice assumes the nature of necessity. Thus *Ibn Máyín eddin Maibedí* relates, in his *Favátah*, "Prolegomena", that the Súfis say: The wished for, but never-found Being proceeds from the field of pure nonentity, and the bare negation puts no foot into the station of evidence and habitation of bodily existence, in the same manner as the wished-for but never-found Being never assumes the color of bodily existence; certainly, the real Being also does not take the color of non-entity. The substance of any thing cannot be caused to vanish into

---

[1] كن فيكون

[2] I think it ought to be *Shabisteri* instead of *Shosteri*, as I find in Baron von Hammer's *Gulshen-raz* (pp. 27–32) a treatise entitled *Hak ol yakin*, as above, attributed to the before quoted Mahmud Shebisteri, of whom more hereafter. The whole title of the abovementioned work is *Hak ol yukin fi mâarifet-i-rebbil âalemin*, "the truth of conviction in the knowledge of the Lord of the world".

[3] The word *yakin* signifies "an intuitive certainty", produced by energy of faith, and not by arguments and proofs.

non-existence; thus, if thou consumest a stick in the fire, its substance is not annihilated although its form changes, and becomes manifest in the form of ashes. The self-existent Being is an essence which is stable in all conditions, and in the accidents of existence, in the forms and states which undergo changes, the divine procreation of the world is the manifested light of his absolute reality, under the shape of divers combinations which thou beholdest.

"Certainly God made the heaven and earth to shine".

In the book of the sagacious is found that the beautiful of this world enjoys the advantage of his beauty, when he beholds and considers its reflexion in a looking-glass; on that account, the absolute Being, having been revealed in the mirror of existences and appropriate places, and having seen his beauty in various mirrors, and in every one of them being exhibited under a shape worthy of himself, become manifest in a series of multitudinous appearances.

The Sufis further say: God is pure, conformable to his essence, above all purity and comparison, and in the gradations of names and attributes praised in both ways. Whoever dispenses with the comparison of something which has no equal, does not know that, declaring God to be without an equal, is comparing him with pure beings. The friends of God say that his name is of three kinds, viz.: he is *itlák*, "absolute", by his essence, or considered as an unsubstantial (abstract) thing;[1] and they give him the name of *zát*, "essence", like that of *kadus*,

---

[1] The original text has here باعتبار امرعدمی *ba itibár-i-amr ádemí*. *Itibar* has in the Dictionary, among other significations, that of "reasoning or computing by comparison; considering with attention; calculating properly", which appears to me the only meaning applicable in this place; *ba itibar* may perhaps here be better interpreted by "in the acceptation (assumption) of". This word occurs twice with امور, *amur* (the plural of *amr*), in the following important passage of *Gulshen raz*:

وجود اندر کالنس حویش ساریست
تعیینها امور اعتباریست
امور اعتباری نیست موجود

"pure, holy"; that is, considered as a substance, he is Being the meaning of which is not dependent upon the meaning of another; they call him *sifet*, "excelling attributes", and *háí*, "living"; that is, considered as a substance, he is a Being whose meaning is dependent upon that of another. They name him *fâl*, "action", like *khálik*, "Creator", which is the general name of God, as well as *rahmen*, "mercy"; but the great name is at last *khafá*, "the concealed (mysterious)". A person asked the lord Shaikh *Bayezíd Bastámí*:[1] "Which is the great name of God?" The Shaikh answered: "Communicate thou to me his least name, that I may give thee in return his greatest": that is to say, the names of God are all great.

عدو بسیار و یکجیزست معدود
جهانرا نیست هستی جز مجازی
سراسر حال او لهوست و بازی

Baron von Hammer interprets *amúri itibarí* by "Gegenstande der Erscheinung", that is "objects of appearance"; I dare differ somewhat in the expression, but not in the meaning of these words: "Existence manifests itself (see p. 29, note 4) in its own place; things perceived by senses are mere objects of acceptation; things of acceptation are not real. There are many numbers, but one only is numbered (that is, numbers are only one unit, repeatedly employed). The world has no existence but as a metaphoric image: its state is entirely a farce and a play".

[1] Bastam is a town of Khorassan, the native place of *Abu Yezid Taifer ben Issa*, one of the most celebrated Súfis of Persia. He had inherited the frock of another mystical personage, called Habib Ajemi. Bastami attained the supreme degree of spirituality — perfect union with God. He occasionally branched out into all the enthusiasm imaginable, saying that God was with him and near him, nay in the sleeve of his garment; and then again he came at times into the regular order of piety and devotion, hoping that God would forgive him his sins, and let his latter end be that of the righteous. It is said of him (see the third *Majalis*, "conference", of Sâdi) that, having once called out to God for union with the supreme Being, he heard the voice from above: "Abu Yezid, thy *thou* is still with thee; if thou wilt come to me, abandon thyself and come". He died in the year of the Hejira 261 (A.D. 874). — (See Transact. of the Lit. Soc. of Bombay, vol. I, p. 100; Malcolm's Hist. of Persia, p. 395; *Pend nameh*, edit. and transl. by Silvestre de Sacy, p. 231.)

The sagacious say: Every era is the epoch of the fame and dominion of a name, and when this epoch expires, it becomes concealed under the name which it had at the epoch of its flourishing state.[1]

They say, the names of the Deity contain the distinct forms in the divine science, and these are called *aâyan sábitah*, "fixed substances",[2] whether general or partial, and these intellectual forms received existence in eternity without beginning, by *fayz*,[3] "emanation", from the essence of God endowed with most holy emanation. Further, the intellectual forms rise into evidence with all dependencies and necessary consequences of the most holy emanation. The fixed substances have a relation to the names of bodies, and to the external substances[4] of

---

[1] Silvestre de Sacy, in the translation of a part of the Definitions of Jorjáni, gives the following note as translated from the Persian (see *Notices et Extraits des MSS.*, vol. X, p. 67): "The Súfis declare that every time is the turn of the manifestation of a name (divine); when the turn of this name is terminated, it conceals itself under another name, for which the turn of denomination is arrived. The periods of the seven planets, each of one thousand years, are attached to it; and the words of the Koran, speaking of God: "*Every day he is in action*, indicate it; *because one day of thy Lord is equivalent to one thousand years of yours*. Verse. *O thou whose light manifests itself in the vest of the world, thy names are manifested in the nature of man; thy science shows itself by the science of* (Muhammed) *the seal* (of prophets), *thy bounty is manifested by the bounty of khatem* (the seal)." The divine names are distinct forms, which are called *aâyan sabitah*, "fixed realities". — (Extracted from the Diván of Ali.)

[2] The word in the text is ازل, *azl*, which means duration of existence during a series of *finite* times, and *infinite* on the side of the *past*, as ابد, *abad*, signifies duration of existence during a series of *finite* times, and *infinite* on the side of the *future*. — (See Definitions of Jorjáni, in *Not. et Ext. des MSS.*, vol. X, p. 39.)

[3] فيض is translated by Silvestre de Sacy "emanation"; and فيض القدس *fayz-al kudis*, by "émanation très sainte" (see *ibid.*, p. 66). In common acceptation, *fayz* signifies "plenty, abundance, bounty, grace"; *fayz-al akdes* means also "communication of divine grace made to angels, prophets, and other superior intelligences without the intervention of the Holy Ghost".

[4] اعيان خارجيه, *aâyan kharjíah*. The scholastics have distinguished fixed and external substances; the Súfis distinguish substances in and without God.

spirits, and between all beings there arises an interposition dependent on the degree of excellence which it has with respect to God. All the reality of accidental beings lies in the external existence; the reality of individuals is dependent upon fixed times, and every one emerges into existence at his time.[1]

The Súfis maintain that all attributes of perfection are necessarily inherent in the supreme holy essence; that is, are fixed by the purity of his essence. What in the accidental substance is fixed by properties, for instance, thy substance, is not sufficient for the revelation of thyself; as long as the attribute of God's essence, which is the principle of that revelation, has not taken firm hold of thee, this revelation cannot be obtained. On the contrary, God, the most High, stands not in need of that revelation of things, on account of the purity which is inherent in him; but his essence is the principle of that revelation; that is, his essence and attributes are one. On this account, the Amir of the believers, Alí, said:

"The perfection of the belief in the unity of God consists in the negation of attributes".

The lord Shaikh Dáud Kaiṡerí says in the *Sherahfes us*, "Commentary upon the bezels":[2] the knowledge of God the most High, in his essence, is the identity of the

---

[1] The word وقت, *wakt*, "time", has a technical signification. — According to Jorjáni, it means: "Your state, that is, that which is required by your actual disposition, and is not produced by design". *Shehab eddin Omar Sohrawerdi* (who died A.D. 1234) says: "*Time* is what dominates man; man is not dominated by any thing more than by his *time*; for time is like a sword, it executes its decrees and cuts. By *time* is therefore meant what comes forcibly upon a man without being the fruit of his action; so that, subject to its power, he is constrained to conform to it. It is said: '*Such a one is under the dominion of time*', that is, he is retired from things which are his own, and transported to things which belong to God".

[2] *Feṡuṡ ol hikem*, "the bezels of philosophy", is one of the most celebrated works composed by Mohí eddin Ibn Arabi, upon whom see a subsequent note. This work was commented, not only by the above-mentioned Daúd Kaiṡerí (of Caesarea), but also by Anifeddin Telmesani, and others. — (See Baron von Hammer's *Geschichte des Osm. Reiches, II[ter] Band Seite* 657.)

essence, and the knowledge of this world is that of the forms of things in it, whether generally or partially; and if one essence is *said to be* the receptacle of manifold things, this *acceptation* is not to be feared, as the things are identic with God according to the acceptation of "existence", and in truth are different *only* according to the acceptation of being either involved or manifested. Further, in reality, there is neither state nor place, but there is one object exhibited under forms of decoration and portraiture by external appearances. *Kaśa*, "God's universal judgment or decree (predestination)" is the summary decision of the conditions of existence, as the decision for the death of all mankind; and *Kadr* is "the interpretation of that decision by determined means, and in consequence of results conformable to the faculties"; for instance, the decision of the death of Záid, on such a day, by such a malady, *Kaśa*, "predestination", is the eternal knowledge concerning existences, and this knowledge is dependent on the *âyán sábitah*, "fixed substances". Each thing demands, by disposition,[1] a peculiar emanation of God.

The Súfis say, according to the sacred text:

"God created man according to his image".

We have the power of acting on account of our being the mirror of the supreme essence; if we say: "The action is ours", it may be right; and if we say: "It is of God", it is equally true. The master of the rose-bower says:

"*Masnavi*. Recognise the mark of God in every place,
Never place the foot without its own limit.
Whoever has a faith other than that of Jabr[2]
Is, according to the word of the prophet, to be accounted a Guéber.

---

[1] استعداد , *istidad*, "disposition", that is, when a thing possesses the near or remote quality for action. — (Jorjání's Definitions.)

[2] The name of *Jabr* is common to several doctors of Muselmanism. The most ancient of them is *Abu Abd-allah Jabr Ben Abd allah al Ansari*, a native of Medina, as it is indicated by his surname. Jabr, according to Mirkhond, first a pagan, after having examined the sacred books of all other nations, Jews and Christians, was vanquished by Muhammed's eloquence, and adopted his faith.

In like manner as that Guéber said: 'Yezdán, Aherman',
So was it as if that ignorant blockhead had said: 'He and me';
The actions have but a metaphorical connection with us,
A connection with him in reality is a ludicrous play.
How came it, O man without intelligence, that, from eternity,
This man should be Muhammed, and the other Abú Jehel?"

It is written in the glorious Koran:
"If any thing good happens to them, they say: 'It comes from God';
and if any thing bad, they say: 'It comes from me'; say: 'Every thing comes from God'."

The Súfis say that the whole heaven is a body, the first intelligence its soul, the breath of the whole his heart, and the spirits of the seven planets, of the fixed stars and the rest, are his power.

"Your creation and your resurrection are as those of one man".

The Shaikh Mohí eddin[1] says in his *Fas hawdí*,

Another Jabr is *Abu Mussa Jabr Ben Haíían al Sufi*, author of the book *Kitab al Jafr*, and of many other, some say five hundred, works upon the philosopher's stone. He lived in the middle of the third century of the Hejira (about A.D. 864).

A third Jabr, an Andalusian, is surnamed *Shems-eddin*.

[1] *Mohi-eddin*, "he who makes religion revive and flourish", is a surname borne by several Muselman doctors. The above-mentioned is *Mohi-eddin Ibn al Arabi*, born in Kordua, in Spain, of an Arabian Family, called *Tayí*, in the year of the Hejira 560 (A.D. 1164). He studied in the academy of Seville, and then visited Asia Minor, Syria, and Egypt, where he heard the most distinguished Shaikhs of his time. He became the founder of a mystic school from which, among other remarkable disciples, the great *Maulana Jelal-eddin Rumi* issued; he is called "the Pole of the mystic world". He died in the year of the Hejira 638 (A.D. 1240), in his seventy-sixth year, and was buried at the foot of mount Cassius, near Damascus, where his sepulchral monument is still well preserved. He left thirty-three works, which are enumerated by Baron von Hammer, the illustrious historian of the Ottoman empire. — (See vol. II, pp. 490, 657 of the German work.)

"chapter of repentance": The world is the image of God, and he the soul and governor of the universe, further he is the great mankind. The Lord Maulavi Jámí, in the *Nakd-al fasus*, "the ready money of bezels", states, that there are two divisions of the beings of the universe: the first consists of those who on no account have any sort of connection with the bodily world, in conformity to office and direction; these, called *Cherubim*, are divided into two classes: the one take not the least notice of the world and its inhabitants, and are named "the great Angels"; the other, although not connected with the bodily world, are yet entranced in astonishment as witnesses and valuers *of God's power*, standing at the curtain of the divine court, and being the ministers of the supreme bounty; before them is an angel entitled "the great spirit", greater than whom no angel exists. According to another interpretation he is said to be "the highest secretary and first intelligence". This great spirit (the blessing of God be upon him!) holds the first rank of this class. The spirit, who is called *Jabríil*, follows after him in this legion.

"The rank which he possesses is a place known".

Another division is composed of those who have connection with the bodily world according to order and office; these are named "spirits", also divided into two classes: the one are spirits who perform their office in the heavens, and these are entitled "the high angels"; the other class are those who perform their office upon earth, and these bear the name of "lower angels". Many thousands of them are appointed to the human race, and many thousands to minerals, to plants, and the animal kingdom. The people of the revelation (prophets) say: "There, where seven angels are not assembled, not a leaf

The Muselmans in India revere, under the name of Mohi-eddin, a saint, son of Zangui and Bibi Fatima, called also Shaikh Saddo. He lived at Sambhal, in Rohilkunt, according to others, at Amroha, in the province of Delhi, where his tomb still exists. There the devotees assemble every year, on the 11th day of the 2nd Rabiâ (the 4th month of the Arabian year) and celebrate the saint's memory, by particular *fatihas*, "prayers", addressed to him, and other acts of devotion. — (See *Mémoire sur les particularités de la Relig. Muselm. dans l'Inde, par M. Garcin de Tassy*, pp. 46–54.)

can germinate from a branch"; the seven angels are meant to be seven divine powers. Thus, the spirits of fire, who are called *Jin* and *Siátín,* "genii and demons", belong to the kind of lower angels, and *Iblis* is their chief and ruler. The lord Shaikh Mahmúd Shósterí says, that Iblis is the power of imagination, which the learned call "the material". The Súfis give it the name of "the foundation of material substance", or *Enka*.[1] According to the Súfis, *matter is mâdum,* "not eternally existent". They call the absolute body "the universal body". The Súfis say, as is found in the *Favátah,* that the spirit of mankind is the absolute spirit of the divinity; thus the spirit of mankind, for the sake of elocution — that is, excellence — expresses itself by sound; and sound, for the sake of elocution, by various distinct modulations, which in utterance are made sensible, becomes a word, and by the combination of words a language acquires reality. The Shaikh Muhammed *Láhaji* says, in his Commentary on *Gulshen raz*,[2] "the Mystery of the Rosebower", that the meaning of the expression "the divine spirit", is "the revelation of truth in the circus of multiplicity", and in the *Sharh mahtas'er,* "abridged Commentary (epitome)" on *Gulshen,* is found that, in like manner as the spirit of mankind becomes sound, and sound a word, so also the divine spirit becomes *jawher,* "substance", and substances become spirits and forms; thus human nature is determined in a manner that its hidden conditions proceed from the interior to manifestation.

The presence of the universal deity, which is expansive in the divine spirit and soul, is fivefold. The first is *hazeret ghaib muílak,* "the presence of the absolute mystery", and

---

[1] See hereafter an explanatory note upon Enka (p. 47).
[2] A work composed by *Mahmud Shebisterí.* His native place was *Shebister,* distant eight parasangs (about twenty-eight miles) from Tabriz, near which place he was buried in A.D. 1320. He wrote the *Gulshen-raz* three years before his death, as an answer to fifteen questions addressed to him by the great Shaikh Hussein, of Khorassan, who died A.D. 1318, one year after the composition of the just-mentioned most celebrated didactical work upon the doctrine of the Súfis.

this is one with the *aâyían sábatah*, "the invariable prototypes (realities of things)". The second is the *hazeret ghaib muśáf*,[1] "the presence of the relative mystery", which is nearest the absolute mystery, and this belongs to pure intellects and spirits. The third is the *hazeret musáf ghaib*,[2] "the presence of the mysterious relation", which is nearest the absolute evidence; this is the world of similitude, or dream. The fourth is the *hazeret shahádet mutlak*,[3] "the presence of the absolute evidence", which reaches from the centre of the earth to the middle of the ninth empyrean heaven. The fifth is the *hazerát jámâh*,[4] "the presence of the vest", and this is the universe in an extensive, and mankind in a restricted, acceptation.[5]

[1] حضرت غيب مضاف.

[2] حضرت مضاف غيب.

[3] حضرت شهادت مطلقه. *Shahádet*, interpreted in common acceptation by "testimony, attestation, witnessing, confession, evidence", is translated by Silvestre de Sacy, in a note of Jorjáni (see a subsequent note), by "assistance". It takes in the terminology of Súfis, a meaning varying according to the particular opinion of their sects; thus it coincides sometimes with "presence", whether with the qualifications of attentive expectation, whether with that of perfect intuition.

[4] حضرت جامعه.

[5] This is a very abstruse doctrine. To throw more light upon it, I shall subjoin the explanation given by Jorjáni upon this subject, according to the French translation of Silvestre de Sacy (see *Not. et Ext. des MSS.*, vol. X, p. 66): "The five divine presences are: 1. *the presence of the absolute absence* (or mystery); its world is the world of *the fixed substances in the scientific presence* (see p. 29, note 6). To the presence of the absolute mystery is opposed: 2. *the presence of the absolute assistance*; its world is that named *Aalem al mulk* (that is, the world of the throne or seat of God, of the four elemental natures); 3. *the presence of the relative absence*; this is divided into two parts: the one, 3. *nearer the presence of the absolute mystery*; the world of which is that of spirits, which belong to what is called *jabrut* and *malkut*, that is, of intelligences and of bare souls; the other: 4. *nearer the presence of the absolute assistance*; and the world of which is that of models (images), called *Aalem al mulkut*; 5. the presence which comprises the four preceding ones; and its world is the world of mankind, a world which reunites all the worlds, and all they contain". This statement differs somewhat from that of our text; to exhibit and to develop, in

The Súfis besides say: The world is life and intellect, as far as the mineral kingdom; but the manifestation of intellect in every body is determined by the temperature of the human constitution. Sometimes bounty attains an excellence which is uttered with ecstasy, and becomes a modulation more powerful than that which strikes the ear: and this is the mode of the prophet (blessing upon him!). Thus is it commonly related that Jabriil brought to the blessed prophet the happy news, that his poor followers will enter heaven five hundred years sooner than the rich. The prophet, full of joy, said: "Can none of you recite a verse?" A person proffered these distichs:
"The serpent of desire bit my heart:
There is, to cure me, neither doctor nor magician,
If not the friend whom I adore:
He alone possesses the theriac and the amulet suitable to my cure".

Upon this the lord prophet, with his companions, moved about in ecstasy, with such a violence that the cloak fell from his shoulder.[1]

Further, the sagacious say that the forms of the sensible world are shades of seeming forms. The Súfis also maintain that a spirit cannot exist without a body;[2] when it breaks forth from a body, it obtains, according to its deeds and actions, an apparent body, which they call *acquired*.

all their variations, the systems of Súfism is far beyond the compass of these notes, and would require a separate work.

[1] Such a tradition existing, we cannot wonder that, from early time to our days, among the religious practices of Durvishes, Súfis, and monastic congregations, there are different kinds of dances, accompanied by song, with or without instrumental music.

[2] The celebrated Leibniz entertained a similar opinion; in consequence of his great principle of *"the sufficient reason"*, he was persuaded that all souls, after death, remain united to an organic whole: "Because", says he, in his *Théodicée* (§ 90), "there is no appearance, that there be, in the order of nature, souls entirely separate from any sort of body". — (See on this subject *La Palingénésie philosophique, par C. Bonnet*, tome II, p. 24 *et seq.*)

SECTION II. — OF THE PROPHETIC OFFICE; AND EXPLANATION OF THE PUBLIC DECLARATIONS CONFORMABLE TO THE REVELATION OF INSPIRED PERSONS

The Súfis say: The prophet is a person who is sent to the people as their guide to the perfection which is fixed for them in the scientific presence (of God) according to the exigency of the dispositions determined by the fixed substances, whether it be the perfection of faith, or another. The Shaikh Hamíd eddin Nagóri[1] states, in his *Sharh-i-ashk*, "Commentary upon Love", that *Abúdíyet*, "devotion",[2] and *rubúbíyet*, "divinity",[3] are both attributes of God; as often as the manifestation of divinity came to seize the lord of the prophetic asylum (Muhammed), and the quality of devotion became effaced in him, in this transitory state,[4] whatever he proffered was the word of God. The Máulaví Mânavi says:

---

[1] In Herbelot's *Bibl. Orient.* we find *Hamid eddin*, a celebrated doctor, surnamed *al Dharir*, "the Blind", disciple of *Kerdori*, and master of *Nassafi the Younger*. The latter died in the year of the Hejira 710 (A.D. 1310). Baron von Hammer, in the catalogue of the literature of the Súfis, annexed to his *Gulshen raz* (p. 32), mentions an *Ishk-namah* "Book of Love", composed by *Ferishte-oghli*.

[2] عبوديت means also "servitude, submission, pious fervour"; it is reckoned one of the most essential qualities of a saint in general. An عبد, *âbid*, is a person continually occupied with religious practices, and all sorts of supererogatory pious acts, with the view of obtaining future beatitude. It may be asked, how can devotion, as said above, be an attribute of God? The answer is that, according to Súfism, God is every thing which appears praise-worthy to man, who can never forsake his own nature. Thus says Sâdi in his fifth Sermon: "A hundred thousand souls, alas! are the devoted slaves of the shoe-dust of that Durvish (God)". He who prays from the inmost of his soul, grants his prayers to himself; he no more prays, but is the God who, at the same time, offers and accepts prayers. — (See *Sufismus*, by F. A. D. Tholuck, p. 155.)

[3] ربوبيت signifies a participation in the nature and excellence of God, attainable by a mortal. There is a school of Súfis, called الحوليت *Alhulíyat*, who think that deity may descend and penetrate into a mortal's mind. Muhammed is supposed to have possessed this eminent quality of a Súfi.

[4] Two technical words occur (among many others) of the Súfis

"As the Koran came from the lips of the prophet,
Whoever asserts, he said not the truth is a Kafr (infidel)".

And when he arrived at the quality of divinity, what he then uttered, this is called by them *hadís*, "sacred saying"; further, what he said with the tongue of divinity, was a *hadís*. The meaning of the words "from *Jabriil*" is this, that between these two qualities (devotion and divinity), is a mind which in the manifestation of divinity is giving information from divinity, but in the quality of divinity there is nothing intervening between itself:[1] hence it is said:

"In love there is no message intervening:
It was itself which acted as its own messenger".

The sagacious Súfís say, that what causes the revelation of the original Being in the gradations of divinity and in the wisdom of a book, and his appearance in whatever form, is the manifestation of his perfection, and this is of two kinds and in a twofold degree. The first degree is manifestation and exhibition in such a manner that whatever exists may prove complete, and this can take place only in the completeness of form; it is man who, according to the terminology of this sect, is indicated by

حال *hal*, and مقام *makám*, which require a particular explanation. *Hál* signifies a feeling of joy or of affliction — of compression or dilatation — or of any other condition, which takes hold of the heart without any effort being made to produce or to provoke it, and which ceases when the soul reverts to the consideration of its own qualities. It is so called whether the same state be repeated or not. I generally render it by "state", above by "transitory state". If it persists and is changed into an habitual faculty, it is then called *makám*; I render it by "station". The *hals* are pure gifts of God; the *makáms* are fruits of labor. The first proceed from God's pure bounty; the second are obtained by dint of efforts. Both words may sometimes be rendered by ecstasy, or ecstatic, supernatural condition, in which the soul loses sight of itself to see God only, and which ceases, as soon as its looks are directed towards itself. — (See *Ext. et Not. des MSS.*, vol. XII, p. 317.)

---

[1] If I understand at all this obscure passage, it means: "there is an immediate connection, without any intervention, between the Deity and man".

it, that is, *essentiality*, which is the union of universalities and particularities: it is said accordingly:

"There is nothing moist — there is nothing dry, that be not in the manifest book (the Koran)". That is: Every thing is contained in the Koran.

Without him (God) there is no strength; it is by him that every thing enters into the area of form and evidence.

"Without thee is nothing in the world;
Ask from thyself, if thou desirest to know what thou art".
"Every thing has an advantage, which, at the junction of its parts, has been placed in it".

The second degree is in the perfection of the existence of forth-bringing and exhibiting; so that every thing which exists, as it exists, is made to appear complete.

The seal, or "the last prophet", in the terminology of this sect, is a person, to whom this office can be appropriated, and from whom the great business may proceed; but, in forthcoming it is not allowed to him to be, in form,[1] all-sufficient in dignity, and in showing this form in the world; this is not confined to a single person; but if this excellence is manifested around, it is acknowledged as *the seal* of dignity in this age. When this condition is established, then, by the before-said interpretation, the moon is said to be the symbol realised in this form, because, in the style of eloquence, it is generally usual to interpret the form of perfection by that of the moon, and "to divide the moon", means in figurative language to elicit thoroughly the sense from this form, without taking into consideration the instruments of imitation and the arrangement of artful contrivances. Thus was it with regard to the promised lord of the prophetic asylum. The lord Imâm Muhammed *núrbakhsh*[2] which he went into a state of trance, which is an intermediate state[1] between sleeping and waking, and on

---

[1] *Suret* signifies the sensible form of a thing; the figure with which it is invested.

[2] *Mír Said Muhammed Nurbaksh* was the assumed name of *Shamseddin*, a descendant from a Guebre family of Irák. He fixed

that account it is said in the first tradition of the ascent:
"I was between sleeping and waking".

And further:
God directed thee in the explanation of things revealed to the prophets and saints, upon whom be peace!"

That his being carried from the mosque of Mecca to the mosque of Jerusalem, is an image of the migration of the terrestrial angels from one place to another. To keep the Imámate (or presidence) during worship is to the prophet an image, that in his religion there are many heirs of the prophet, who are the saints and learned men of the age.

Borák, the vehicle of devotion, is like an image of prayer; the saddle and bridle represent the ready mind and the perfect union of religion. The members of Borák, of precious jewels, typify purity, candor, affection, submission, humility, and perfect love of God, rejecting all other desire except that tending towards the supreme Being in prayer. The restiveness of Borák, and the aid given by Jabríil in mounting Borák present a similitude of the reluctance of the human mind to the wisdom of its knowledge of God, and Jabríil figures the science of divinity.

The *travelling by steps up to heaven*, means the gradual elevation by steps, which are remembrance, rosary-beads, praising and magnifying by exclamation, God and the like, by which the heart arrives from this nether world of sensuality to the upper world.

By *the first heaven*, which is that of the moon, is understood the arrival at the station of cordiality. The opening of the heavenly door by an angel, and the appearance of Jabríil, is figuratively the victory of the heart over

himself in Kachmir, where he became the founder of a sect which acknowledged him as a prophet and a *Mahdi*, and took from him the name of *Nur-bakshian*. — (See *Journal des Savants*, avril 1840; article de M. Mohl sur *l'Histoire de Ferishta*.)

[1] The word here used by the author is برزخ *barzakh*, "interval of time, according to the Koran (chap. XXIII) between the death of a man and the resurrection, before which the souls of the departed receive neither reward nor punishment".

remembrance, as will be explained in the sequel. The arriving at the heaven of *Aí áred*, "Mercury", is the image of elevation on the regions of cordiality on account of meditation on the knowledge of God, as —

"One hour's meditation is preferable to seventy years of exterior worship".

The arrival at the heaven of *Zaherah*, "Venus", signifies elevation of the upper angels, on account of the delight and beatitude which are produced in the interior by the love of God. The arrival at the heaven of the *sun* is to be interpreted as the elevation in the inner sense, on account of accomplishing the precepts of the faith, and the promulgated orders, which are derived from it. The arrival at the heaven of *Meríkh*, "Mars", denotes the elevation which may have taken place in consequence of the war made upon the spirit of fraud. The arrival at the heaven of *Mishterí*, "Jupiter", offers an image of the elevation on account of purity, piety, and abstinence from any thing doubtful, which are manifested by these steps. The arrival at the heaven of *Zehel*, "Saturn", is to be understood as the elevation from the state of spirituality to that of mystery by the blessing of exertion and sanctity, by choice or by force, which means overcoming a difficulty.

The arrival at *Falek sábetab*, "the heaven of the *fixed stars*", is an image of the elevation by the blessing of firmness in the faith, and evident proof of diligent permanency in good practices, and fidelity in the love of God and of the people of God. The arrival at *Falek atlas*, "the *crystalline sphere*", is to be interpreted as the elevation to the utmost boundary of the angels by the blessing of interior purity, and a heart free from all desire except that after God.

The *remaining behind of Borák*, the *arch*, and *Jabríil*, in each station indicate the meaning, that in the worlds of the upper spirits, and the empyreal heaven, there are certain extents of spiritual faculties, and limits of imagination, so that no body can deviate from the station of comprehension, and

"The place of his acquisition is a place known".

The explanation of this is, that, as the elemental body cannot deviate from the elemental world, and the soul, however composed it may be, cannot make a step out of the nether dominion, as well as the heart cannot leave the outer skirts of the upper angelic courts, so that the mystery never comes forth from the middle of the upper dominion, and the spirit cannot make a step out of the extreme ends of the upper regions into the *âalem-i-jabrût*, "the highest empyreal heaven", and the hidden cannot transgress the empyreal world. Hence proceeds the sense of *ghaib al ghaiyûb*, "evanescence of evanescences", the *mysterious* hidden.

The *Enka*, upon the mount *Kâf*,[1] is divinity, and there

---

[1] We have already mentioned the *Enka*, or *Simurgh*, "thirty birds", as an object of fabulous romance. At one time this mysterious bird was counsellor of the Jins (genii), and for the last time was visible at the court of Solomon, the son of David, after which he retired to the mount *Kaf*, which encircles the earth. According to a tradition of Muhammed, God created, in the time of Moses, a female bird, called *Enka*, having wings on each side and the face of a man. God gave it a portion of every thing, and then created a male of the same species. They propagated after the death of Moses, feeding on ferocious beasts and carrying away children, until the intervening time between Jesus and Muhammed, when, at the prayer of Khaled, this race was extinguished. Proverbially, the Enka is mentioned as a thing of which every body speaks without having ever seen it.

But a much greater import is attached to this name in the doctrine of the Sufis: with them this bird is nothing less than the emblem of the supreme Being, to be sought with the utmost effort and perseverance through innumerable difficulties which obstruct the road to his mysterious seat. This idea was ingeniously allegorized in the famous poem entitled *Mantek al tair*, "the colloquy of the birds", composed by *Ferid-eddin Attar*, a Persian poet, who was born in Kerken, a village near Nishapúr, in the year of the Hejira 513 (A.D. 1119), and lived 110, 112, or 115 years, having died in A.H. 627, 629 or 632 (A.D. 1229, 1231 or 1234). In this composition, the birds, emblems of souls, assemble under the conduct of a hoopoe (*upapa*), their king, in order to be presented to Simurgh. To attain his residence, seven valleys are to be traversed; these are: 1. the valley of research; 2. that of love; 3. that of knowledge; 4. of sufficiency (competence); 5. of unity; 6. of stupefaction; and 7. that of poverty and annihilation, beyond which nobody can proceed; every one is annihilation into God. He does not allow plurality nor partnership of eternal beauty and strength, and from that exalted station there is no descent. When a bird or man is annihilated, a name is always without a designate object. *Vás el*, "the perfect master of union",[1] finds in this

finds himself attracted without being able to advance. These are evidently as many gradations of contemplative life, and austere virtue, each of which is described in glowing terms, for which scarce an equivalent is to be found in European languages. The birds, having attained the residence of Simurgh, were at first ordered back by the usher of the royal court, but, as they persevered in their desire, the violence of their grief met with pity. Admitted to the presence of Simurgh, they heard the register of their faults committed towards him read to them, and, sunk in confusion, were annihilated. But this annihilation purified them from all terrestrial elements; they received a new life from the light of majesty; in a new sort of stupefaction, all they had committed during former existence was cancelled, and disappeared from their hearts; the sun of approximation consumed, but a ray of this light revived them. Then they perceived the face of Simurgh: "When they threw a clandestine look upon him, they saw thirty birds in him, and when they turned their eyes to themselves, the thirty birds appeared one Simurgh: they saw in themselves the entire Simurgh; they saw in Simurgh the thirty birds entirely". They remained absorbed in this reflection. Having then asked the solution of the problem *We* and *Thou*, that is, the problem of apparent identity of the divinity and his adorers, they received it, and were for ever annihilated in Simurgh: the shade vanished in the sun. — (See *Notices et Extraits des MSS.*, vol. XII, pp. 306–312.)

According to the thirty-seventh and last allegory of *Azz-eddin Elmocadessi*, an Arabian poet, who died in A.H. 678 (A.D. 1280), the assembled birds resolved to pass a profound sea, elevated mountains, and consuming flames, to arrive at a mysterious island where *Simurgh* or *Enka maghreb*, "the wonderful", resided, whom they wished to choose for their king. After having supported the fatigues, and surmounted the difficulties and perils of their voyage, they attained their aim, a delightful sojourn, where they found every thing that may captivate the senses. But when they offered their homage to Simurgh, he at first refused them, but having tried their perseverance in their attachment to him, he at last gratified their desire, and granted them ineffable beatitude. — (See *Les Oiseaux et les Fleurs*, Arabic text and French translation, by M. Garcin de Tassy, pp. 119, etc., and notes, p. 220.)

[1] The Súfís are divided into three great classes, to wit: 1. و اصلان *vásilán*, "those who arrived (at the desired end)", the

station by annihilation into God emancipation from the confinement of visible existence, and acquires with an eternal mansion the intimate connection with God, and an exit from the garment of servitude, and becomes endowed with divine qualities. In the station of transition into God, Jabríil is the image of wisdom and of manifest knowledge, on which account it has been declared —
> "There are moments when I am with God in such a manner that neither angel nor archangel, prophet nor apostle, can attain to it".

When at the time of transition, science, comprehension, knowledge, and all qualities are cancelled and vanish, then transitory knowledge unites with the perfect science, the dangers of mankind are carried off and disappear, before the rays of light of the supreme Being. And this is the kind of knowledge which Jabríil revealed. Above this station resides the absolute Being. Again, ascent and descent, and letter and sound denote the meaning that mankind comprises all qualities — the high and the low; by the exigency of its united properties, at times drowned in the ocean of unity, man is bewildered; and, at times, yielding to this prevailing nature, he associates with women. Know what Shaikh Aziz Nasfy says: Men, devoted to God's unity declared, regarding the expression *táí asmavat*, "the folding up heaven", that "heaven" signifies something that is high and of a bountiful expansion[1] with respect to those who are below it, and this, causing a bountiful communication, may take place either in the spiritual or in the material world; the bestower of the bountiful com-

---

[1] فيص Silvestre de Sacy translates "emanation, overflowing". — (*Journal des Savans, déc.*, 1821, p. 733.)

nearest to God: 2. سالكان *sálikan*, "the travellers, the progressive"; 3. مقيمان *mukíman*, "the stationaries". — According to others (see Graham, Transact. of the Lit. Soc. of Bombay, vol. I, pp. 99, 100), a Súfí may be: 1. a *salik*, "traveller"; 2. a مجذوب *majezub*, "one attracted in a state of intoxication from the wine of divine love"; 3. a *majezub salik*, "an attracted traveller", that is, a partaker of the above two states. I omit other divisions and subdivisions.

munication may be from the latter, he may be from the former, world. Further, any thing may be either *terrestrial* or *heavenly*. If thou hast well conceived the sense of the heavenly and terrestrial, know that mankind has four *nishá*, "stages",[1] in like manner as the blasts of the trumpet are four times repeated: because death and life have four periods. In the first stage, man is living under the form of a thing; but, with respect to qualities and reason, he is a dead thing. In the second stage, under the form of mind, he is a living thing, but, with respect to qualities and reason, a dead thing. In the third stage, under the form of mind, qualities he is a living thing, but, with respect to reason, a dead thing. In the fourth stage, under the form of mind and qualities, and reason, he is a living thing. In the first stage, he is entirely in the sleep of ignorance, darkness, and stupidity, as

"Darkness upon darkness ——"

In this stage he awakes from the first sleep; in the second stage, from the second; in the third, from the third sleep; in the fourth stage, from the last sleep; and in this awaking of the heart he becomes thoroughly and entirely awake, and acquires perfect possession of himself, and knows positively that all he had known in the three preceding stages was not so: because truth, having been but imaginary, was falsehood; and that heaven and earth, as they had been understood before, were not so. Further, in this stage, earth will not be that earth, and heaven not that heaven, which men knew before. This is the meaning of the words:

> "On the day when the earth shall be changed into something else than the earth, as well as the heaven, and when all that shall be manifested by the power of God, the only one, the Almighty".[2]

And when they arrived at that station and possessed positively the form of mind, qualities, and reason of an individual, certainly they knew by means of revelation and inspiration, that except one there is no being, and

---

[1] نشا is interpreted in the dictionary: growing, producing, being borne upward, etc.; above it can but signify "a condition of being".

[2] Koran.

this being is God, the glorious and sublime; they were informed of the real state of things from the beginning to the utmost extremity. In the account concerning the obscuration of the moon, and sun, and stars, they said: that stars have their meaning from the beginning of the light, which is produced in the hearts of the intelligent and select; that the sun denotes the utmost fulness and universality of light; and that the moon, a mediator between the sun and the star,[1] from all sides, spreads their tidings. Then the sun is the universal bestower of abundant blessings; the moon is in one respect "a benefactor", in another respect, "benefitted". As often as the sun's light, which is the universal light, manifests and spreads itself, unity of light comes forth; the light of the moon and that of the stars is effaced by the light of the sun. From the beginning, the prophet says, that —

"When the stars shall fall,
And in the midst,
"When the moon shall be obscured",
And when the select associate with the bestower of abundant blessings, that
"When the sun and moon shall unite",
there remains no trace of *istifáset*, "diffusion", nor of *afáset*,[2] "profusion".
"When the sun shall be folded up".

It was said that the earth of the last judgment signifies that earth on which the creatures of the world will be assembled, and that earth is the existing mankind, because the permanence of all beings is not possible upon any other earth. Further, there will be the day of the last judgment, and the presence of the inhabitants of the world is not intended, nor possible, upon any other earth but the actual earth of mankind. Moreover there will be Friday,[3] and truth will be separated from falsehood upon no other earth but upon the earth of the actual mankind.

---

[1] In the Desátir the moon is called "the key of heaven".
[2] استفاضت and افاضت.
[3] The weekly holiday of the Muhammedans.

Then, there will be the day of the last judgment, and no mystery among mysteries will be manifested upon any other earth but that of actual mankind. Afterwards, there will be the day of ripping open the secrets, and upon no earth will a retribution be given to any body but upon the earth of the actual mankind. Finally, there will be the day of faith.

The lord durvish Sabjány gave the information, saying: With the Súfí's heaven is beauty; certainly the other world of objects of beauty is to be referred to the beauty of God; and in hell there is majesty;[1] necessarily the other world of objects of majesty is referrable to that of God; and the *Jelálían*, or "those to whom majesty applies", will be satisfied in like manner as the *Jemálian*, "those to whom beauty appertains".[2] Further, it is said, hell is the place of punishment; this means that if an object of beauty be joined to majesty, it becomes disturbed; in like manner majesty is made uneasy by beauty. From the lord Sabjáni comes also the informa-

---

[1] جلال *jelál*, "glory, majesty". I suppose "terrific majesty" may be understood. We find, in Richardson's Dictionary, that a sect called *Jelálíyat*, followers of *Said Jelál Bokhari*, worship the more terrible attributes of the deity.

[2] This is an obscure passage. Silvestre de Sacy (*Journal des Savants*, janvier, 1822, p. 13) says: "I see by the Dabistán that, by means of allegory, the Súfís destroy the dogma of eternal punishment, as they destroy what concerns Paradise; but this subject is touched upon but in a superficial manner in the Dabistán, p. 486. . . . I confess, as to the rest, that I have not yet formed to myself a very clear idea of this theory". He subjoins the following note: "Paradise, according to the Dabistán is, with the Súfís, 'the beauty of God', جمال *jemal*, and hell, 'the glory', جلال *jelal*; men who, by their conduct, belong to the last attribute of the divinity, which is designated under the name of hell; that is the جلالیان *jelalian*, find pleasure in it, and when it is said that hell is a place of torment, this means that those who belong to the attribute of beauty, the جمالیان *jemalían*, would be unfortunate, if they should be placed in the situation of those who belong to the attribute of glory, the جلالیان ; the same would be the case with those who belong to the attribute of glory, or to hell, if they should experience the destiny of those who belong to the attribute of beauty, or of Paradise".

tion that the sagacious declare: Phârâoh was worthy of the name of God, and in him the establishment of divinity gained predominance, as well as in Moses the establishment of divine mission. On that account the lord Imám of the professors of divine unity, the Shaikh *Mahíeddin* gave in several of his compositions the proof of Pharáoh's faith, and declared him to be a worthy object *of veneration*, as well as Moses. It is said also, that the land of Arafat[1] signifies the land, which is sought by those who made a vow, and conceived the desire, of pilgrimage, and with their face turned towards this land, with the utmost effort and endeavor proceed upon their way and journey; if in this country they meet with the day of *Arirfah*, that is, "the ninth day of the moon", and accomplish the pilgrimage, they are then considered as having become pilgrims, and to have found the fruit of their journey, and fulfilled their desire, as is said:

"He who reaches the mount Arafah has accomplished the pilgrimage".

If they have not arrived in this land on the said day, they have not accomplished the pilgrimage, they have not become pilgrims nor fulfilled their desire. If this matter be well understood, it necessarily follows that the land of Arifát signifies the actual earth of mankind, because all beings, heavenly and earthly, are upon the way of travelling, until they arrive at the dignity of

---

[1] Arafat is a mountain not far from Mecca. Muhammedans believe that Adam and Eve, having been separated to perform penance, searched for each other during a hundred and twenty or two hundred years, until at last they met again upon the mountain *Arafah*, the name of which is derived from the Arabian verb "to know". This is one of the etymologies of this name; I omit others relating to Abraham (see D'Ohsson, t. II, pp. 83–86). This mountain, in the pilgrimage to Mecca, is one of the principal sacred stations, which the pilgrims cannot enter without having taken the *Ihhram*, or "penitential veil", on the first day of the moon *Zílhajah* (the last of the Arabian year); on the 9th day of the same month, called also *yum-Arafah*, "the day of knowledge", they arrive at Arafah, where they perform their devotions until after sunset, and then proceed to Mecca to execute the sacred rites.

mankind, and when they arrive at it, their journey and voyage is accomplished. If on this earth, which is that of the actual mankind, they arrive on the day of Aráfat, which means the knowledge of God, they have attained their wish at the Kâbah, they have accomplished their pilgrimage, and become pilgrims.

Haj, in the Dictionary, is interpreted *kaśed*, "aspiring to", and *kaśed*, in the law, means the house which Ibrahim the prophet (the blessing of God be upon him!) built in Mecca, and, in truth, this means the house of God, according to these words:

"Neither the earth nor the heavens can contain me, but only the heart of the believing servant".

Besides, the Mobed says:

"At the time of prayer the dignity of man is shown;
Profit by this time, as perhaps fate may seize it".

The sagacious Súfís said: Every action of the actions commanded by law denotes a mystery of the mysteries. *Ghasel*, "bathing", means coming forth by resignation from foreign dependence. *Waśu*, "ablution", indicates abandonment of great occupations. *Mazmaza*, "rinsing the mouth", refers to the rapture caused by the sweetness of remembrance. *Istinsak*,[1] "washing the nostrils three times, by inhaling water out of the palm of the hand", denotes inhaling the perfumes of divine bounty. *Istinsar*, "drawing up water through the nostrils and discharging it again", signifies throwing off blameable qualities. *Washing the face*, has the meaning of turning our face to God. *Washing the hand* is withholding the hand from prohibited things. *Washing the feet* has reference to giving precedence to diligence upon the carpet of devotion. *Standing upright* signifies experience in the earthly station. *To be turned towards the Kiblah* is a sign of offering supplications to the divine majesty. *Joining both hands* denotes the bond of an obligatory engagement. *Keeping the hands open during prayers* means holding back the hand from all except what relates to God. The *Takbír*,[2] "pious ex-

---

[1] See D'Ohsson's *Tableau général de l'Empire Othoman*, tom. II, p. 16.
[2] The *Takbir* consists of these words: *Allah 'u akbar, Allah 'u akbar,*

clamation", signifies respect to divine commands. *Ker* *chanting* (the Koran or prayers), is perusing the divine signets upon the tables of fate, preserved in the heart by means of the interpretation of the tongue, and the renewal of information upon the boundaries of commanded and prohibited things. *Rukuâ*, "bowing the head with the hands upon the knees", represents the state of resignation and submission. *Sajûd*, "prostration",[1] indicates investigation of the divine Being, and dismissal of all pretension. *Tashahhud*, "ritual profession of religion", refers to the state of resignation and humility. *To sit down and to stand up before God five times* means understanding and appreciating the five majesties, which are: divinity, grandeur, dominion, power, and love of humanity. *Two rikâts*,[2] "attitudes of devotion in the morning", are indicative of God's absolute being and of reality. *Four rikâts* relate to four effulgencies, which are impressiveness, agency, inherence of attributes, and substantiality. *Three rikâts*, imply separation, union, and union of unions, viz.: *separation*, in viewing the creatures without God; *union*, in viewing God without the creatures; and *union of unions*, in viewing God in the creatures, and the creatures in God;

la ilahi ill' Allah, Allah 'u akbar, Allah 'u akbar, va l'illah 'il hamd, "God, most high! God, most high! there is no God but God! God most high! God most high! praises belong to God. — (D'Ohsson, vol. II, p. 77.)

[1] The prostration is made with the face to the earth, that is, the knees, toes, hands, nose, and forehead touching the ground. During the prostration the *takbir* is recited.

[2] Several prescribed attitudes and practices constitute the *namaz*, or "prayer": 1. The Muselman stands upright, his hands raised to the head, the fingers separated, and the thumbs applied to the inferior part of the ears; 2. he places his hands joined upon the navel; 3. bows the upper part of his body, and, the hands upon his knees, keeps it horizontally inclined; 4. places himself in the second attitude; 5. prostrates himself as described in the preceding note; 6. raises the upper part of his body, and, kneeling, sits upon his legs, the hands placed upon his thighs; 7. makes a second prostration; 8. rises, and stands as in the second attitude. These eight attitudes, during which he recites several times the before-quoted *takbir*, form a *rikât*. — (See D'Ohsson, vol. II, pp. 77 *et seq*.)

so that the view of the one may not to the heart be a veil to the view of the other. *Keeping the fast* refers to the purity of the interior. *The sight of halál,* "the new moon",¹ is seeing the eye-brows of the perfect spiritual guide. *Aíd,* "a feast", is the knowledge of God. *Kurban,* "sacrificing"² (killing victims), denotes annihilating the brutal spirit. *Rozah,* "fasting",³ has three degrees. The first degree is guarding the belly and the sexual organs from what is improper; the second degree is guarding one's self from unbecoming words and deeds; the third degree is

---

¹ The apparition of the new moon is to the Muhammedans an important phenomenon, as it marks the beginning of their fasts, feasts, and other religious practices, which, to be valid, must be observed exactly at the prescribed time. On that account, the magistrates in the Musulman empire are attentive to announce the right epoch; the *Muezins,* or "cryers", of the highest mosques, at the approach of the new moon pass the whole night on the top of the minarets to observe the precise moment. Thus, the fast of the *Ramazan,* which lasts thirty days, begins at the apparition of the new moon; the commencement of the moons *Shewel* and *Zilhijah* are important for the celebration of the two only feasts in the Muhammedan year: the first is the *âid-fitr,* "the feast of breaking fast", which occupies one or three days, and seventy days after this is the *âid-kurban,* "the feast of sacrifice", which lasts four days: thus the grave Muselmans allow but seven days of their whole year to festivity. As their years are lunar, these two feasts run in the space of thirty-three years through all the seasons of the year. — (D'Ohsson, tome II, p. 227; tome III, pp. 4–5, and elsewhere.)

² The immolation of an animal in honor of the Eternal on the prescribed day is of canonical obligation: every Muselman, free, settled, and in easy circumstances, is bound to offer in sacrifice a sheep, an ox, or a camel. Several persons, to the number of seven may associate for such a purpose. To this is added the distribution of alms to the poor, consisting of killing one or more animals, sheep, lambs, goats, to be dressed, a part of which is tasted by the sacrificer and his family, and the rest given to the poor. (*Ibid.,* t. II, p. 425.)

³ Fasting, with the Muhammedans, imposes an entire abstinence from all food whatever, and a perfect continence during the whole day from the first canonical hour of morning, which begins at daybreak, until sunset. There are different sorts of fasts; canonical, satisfactory, expiatory, votive, and supererogatory. Each of them, although determined by different motives, requires, nevertheless, the same abstinence during the whole day. — (*Ibid.,* t. III, p. 1.)

guarding the heart from whatever is contrary to God. *Jahad*, "holy war upon unbelievers", signifies combating the spirit of deceit. *Múmen*, "right faith", implies adherence to whatever is essential to the true worship of God, and tendency to it by any way which God wills, for —
> "The road towards the idols is formed of the great number of sighs of the creatures".

The lord *Aín ul-Kazat* said, he has learned upon his way, that the essence of all creeds is God, and that of all creeds of the sophists is this:
> "All shall perish except his countenance (that is God's); all that is upon the earth is perishable".

And the meaning of the verse of the merciful is, that at a certain time he will be nothing, because on that very day all is nothing; and this very opinion is the principal part of the creed of sharp-sighted men. In the *tikwiyat mâni*, "the strengthening of sense", the lord *Aín ul Kazat, saheb-i zúkí*, "possessor of delight", said that the mood of the verbal noun is in progressive efficiency at all times, whilst perdition of all things at all times is also constant, but has no determined future time: consequently this perdition, which is an indetermined tense, does not imply that the contingent efficiency is perdition in a future time.

The Imám *Muhammed Núr bakhsh* stated, that all those who are reckoned to have seen God as particular servants near to him, have said the truth; because the rational spirit, which means that of mankind, is pure and uncompounded; on that account it is not prevented from seeing God, and those who speak against the sight are also right, because the eye cannot see the mysterious blessed Being on account of his solitude. An investigator of truth has said: Those who assert the solitude of God are right: because the blessed Being is solitary. And those who speak of his corporeity, and consider God as one of the bodies, such as fire, air, water, or earth, say right, because he is in every sort of beings. Likewise, those who hold him to be good or bad, are not wrong; because nothing exists without him, so that what happens can happen but by his order. And those who ascribe the bad to themselves are right, because in practice they are the movers of their works. So it is with other opinions, such as those who consider God as a Father with regard to all existing beings, and this opinion is true.

The Sonnites recognise Abu Bekr (may God reward him), as a khalif on the strength of his perfection: this is sufficiently founded. But the Shíâhs oppose that on the supposition of his deficiencies. Besides, everybody may, conformably to his own conceptions, have some objection to Abu Bekr. In the same manner, concerning the future state, there are contradictory creeds of nations, and histories of their princes in the world adopted as certain. All these contradictions of the inhabitants of this world are to be considered in this point of view — that they are *more or less* belonging to truth.

The Súfís maintain that *vilayet*, "holiness",[1] in the Dictionary signifies vicinity (to God), and in the public circle to be chosen by the people of God, is evident prophetic mission, and interior faith is incitement to prophecy; the prophet is its faith, and the incitement of the faith of a

---

[1] A possessor of velayet, a *veli*, "a saint", according to Jámi (in the Lives of Súfís) is destined to serve as an instrument for manifesting the proof of prophetic mission. Extraordinary powers over all nature are ascribed to such a man. According to the *Kashef ul mahjub*, "the revelations of the veiled being", composed by Shaikh *Ali Osman Ben Ebil-Ali el Ghaznavi*, there are four thousand saints in the world, walking separate from each other upon the ways of God. Among these, the first three hundred are called *Akhyár*, "the best"; the next four hundred are the *Abdal*, commonly called "Santons"; after them seven hundred *Ebrar*, "just men"; further, four hundred *Awtad*, "posts or stakes"; finally, three hundred *Nukeba*, "chosen". According to the author of *Futuhat-i-Mekkí*, "the revelations of Mecca", that is, Mahi-eddin Muhammed, before-mentioned (p. 37, note 1), there exist at any time seven *Abdal*, or Saints, who preside the seven terrestrial zones, or climates. Each of them, in his climate, corresponds to one of the seven prophets in the following order: Abraham, Moses, Aaron, Edris, Joseph, Jesus and Adam, who reside in so many heavenly spheres. To the said Abdal belong the *Oweis*, that is the great shaikhs, and pious men who, nourished in the prophet's lap, are never tainted by age.

saint is the mission of a prophet, and the faith of an apostle is the completion of the apostleship. Inspiration takes place without the intervention of an angel, and revelation with the intervention of an angel is the revelation appropriate to the prophet. Inspiration is also appropriate to him.

The pious Sajan Sajání says, the perfection of sanctity is the period of a *Mahdí's* time; hence all those among the saints who claimed the dignity of a Mahdi, were divine. In the same manner as every malady of the body has a curative medicine, so every malady of the spirit has also its means of cure. Thus, as the pulse and the urine are indicative of the state of bodies, so dream and vision indicate the state of the spirit. On that account, the devotees relate the visions to their Shaíkh, who is the doctor of the soul.

The Súfís say, that upon the way of pilgrimage there are seven *mertebah*, "degrees". The first degree consists of penitence, obedience, and meditation, and in this degree the light is, as it were, green. The second degree is *the purity of the spirit* from satanic qualities, violence, and brutality; because, as long as the spirit is the slave of satanic qualities, it is subject to concupiscence, and this is the quality of fire. In this state Iblis evinces his strength, and when the spirit is liberated from this, it is distressed with the quality of fierceness, which may be said *flashing*, and this is comfortable to the property of wind. Then it becomes insatiable,[1] and this is similar to water. After this it obtains quietness, and this quality resembles earth.[2] In the degree of repose, the light is as it were blue, and the utmost reach of one's progress is the earthly dominion. The third degree is *the manifestation of the heart*, by laudable qualities, which is similar to red light, and the utmost reach of its progress is the middle of the upper dominion; and in this station the heart praises

---

[1] The text has ملحمة *malhamah*, which means "gluttonous, eager after any thing to excess"; if *mulhim*, it means "inspired".

[2] The ecstatic conditions desired by the Súfís are attainable only in a perfect apathy, that is, in a cessation of all action of the corporeal organs and intellectual faculties.

God, and sees the light of worship and spiritual qualities. With the pure Súfís, "the heart" signifies the form of moderation which keeps the mind in such dispositions that it may not at all be inclined to any side towards excess and redundancy, and the possessor of his mind whose fortunate lot is such a station, is praised as "the master of the heart", or "the lord of the mind". The fourth degree is the *applying of the constitution to nothing else but to God*, and this is similar to yellow light, and the utmost reach of its progress is the midst of the heavenly *malkut*, "dominion". The fifth degree of the soul is that *which resembles white light*, and the utmost aim of its progress is the extreme heavenly dominion. The sixth degree is *the hidden*, which is like a black light,[1] and the utmost reach of its progress is the *âálemi jabrút*, "the world of power". The seventh degree is *ghaiyúb al ghaiyúb*, "the evanescence of evanescence",[2] which is *faná*, "annihilation", and *baka*, "eternal life", and is colorless; this is absorption in God, non-existence, and effacement of the imaginary in the true being, like the loss of a drop of water in the ocean; and "eternal life" is the union of the drop with the sea, and abstraction from all except the proper view of the heart, or separation from the idle images which prevented the *salik*, "traveller", in the midst of existence from distinguishing the drop from the

---

[1] According to the Dict., *Ferhengi Shuuri* (vol. II, p. 430, edit. of Constantinople) the seven heavens mentioned in these pages as habitations of the perfect are called *Heft-aureng*, "seven thrones" (a name commonly given to the seven stars of the Great Bear); they have seven colors, the highest is the black.

[2] غيوب الغيوب. Silvestre de Sacy translates it, *la disparition de la disparition*, "the disappearance of disappearance", that is to say, *perfect absorption*. We have (p. 40, note 3) met with the term *hazeret*, "presence", which is a qualification either of attentive expectation, or perfect intuition; opposite to this we find *ghaib*, "absence, disappearance, evanescence": this is a station attainable only to a *vali*, "saint", by means of *jamah*, "union", when he sees nothing else but God and his unity; this station coalesces with *faná*, "annihilation", when his personal existence is withdrawn from his eyes, and he acquires *baka*, "eternal and sole life with and in God".

ocean. *Faná*, "annihilation", is of two kinds: partial, and universal. The partial consists in this: that a traveller is effaced at once, or that, by gradation, several of his members are effaced, and then the rest of his members. The senses and faculties pass first through the exigency of *sukr*, "intoxication", and, secondly, through that of *sahu*, "recovery from ebriety". The universal annihilation consists in this: that all existences belonging to the worlds of *malik, malkut,* and *jabrút,* "of the angels, of dominion, and power", are effaced at once, or by gradation: first, the three kingdoms of nature are effaced; then the elements; further the heavens; afterwards, *malkut,* "dominion"; finally, *jabrut,* "power". Proceeding, the traveller experiences first the exigency of a sudden manifestation[1] of majesty, and, secondly, that of beauty.

The author of this book heard from the durvish Sabjání, that what the prophet has revealed, viz.: "*that earth and heaven will go to perdition*", signifies "annihilation", not as people take it in the common acceptation, but in a higher sense, "annihilation in God"; so that God with all his attributes manifests himself to the pious person, who becomes entirely annihilated. Eternal life, which is the opposite of annihilation, has also four divisions. The first degree is eternal existence with God, when the pious person from the absorption in God returns, and sees

---

[1] The word used in the original is تجلى *tajelí*, signifying here properly "a sudden burst upon the eyes, a transitory vision". This word occurs, evidently with this meaning, in the following passage of Sâdi's *Gulistan*, "Rose-garden", (chap. II, tale 9), which at the same time elucidates the state of the Súfí above alluded to: "The vision (of God) which the pious enjoy, consists of manifestation and occultation; it shows itself, and vanishes from our looks", — VERSE. *Thou showest thy countenance and thou concealest it. Thou enhancest thy value and sharpenest our fire. When I behold thee without an intervention, it affects me in such a manner that I lose my road. It kindles a flame, and then quenches it by sprinkling water; on which account you see me sometimes in ardent flames, sometimes immersed in the waves.*

There are different sorts of تجليات *tajelíat,* "manifestations", and whenever the mystic has attained the first degrees of such divine favors, he receives no more his subsistence but by supernatural ways.

himself *âyin vajud*, "a real being", endowed with all qualities —

"Who has seen himself, saw God".

If in absorption he keeps consciousness, there remains duality behind.

In the abridged commentary upon *Gulshen raz*, it is stated, that there are four kinds of manifestations. The first is *ásárí*, "impression", by which the absolute being appears under the form of some corporeal beings, among which the human form is the most perfect. The second kind is *Afâalí*, "belonging to action", when the contemplative person sees the absolute being endowed with several attributes of action, such as creator, or nourisher, and the like, or sees himself a being endowed with one of the attributes. The manifestations are frequently colored with lights, and exhibit all sorts of tints. The third kind is *sifátí*, "belonging to attributes", when the contemplative person sees the absolute being endowed with the attributes of his own essence, such as science and life, or sees himself a real being, endowed with these attributes. The fourth kind is *zatí*, "essence", in which, on account of manifestation, annihilation takes place, so that the possessor of this manifestation participates in a condition in which no trace of himself remains, and no consciousness whatever is preserved. It is not necessary that the manifestation be colored in a vest of light, or that every light be a light of manifestation. It may happen that a light proceeds from a prophet, a saint, or a creature. The symptom of manifestation is annihilation, or the science (that is intimate knowledge) of the object manifested at the time of manifestation. The evidence for the truth of manifestations is derived from the Koran, or from traditions.

"I am God, the Lord of creatures".

Moses heard the voice from a bush,[1] and the chosen prophet said:

---

[1] The bush from whence Moses heard the voice of God is mentioned in the Commentary upon the Koran in the following manner. Moses, travelling with his family from Midian to Egypt, came to the

"I saw my Lord under the most excellent form".

The writer of these pages heard from the durvish Sabjáni that the Hindus and other nations, having formed and adored as Gods various different images, this is founded upon the fact, that eminent persons among them were impressed with manifestations; and in such a manner the ten ávatárs became the counterfeits of these manifestations; some of the ávatárs held themselves to be divinities, because they have been the masters of these manifestations; that the Jews and other nations acknowledge God under bodily forms proceeds from the like manifestations. Besides, that Pharâoh declared himself to be a God, comes from a like manifestation:[1] because Pharaoh, under his own form had seen God; on

valley of Towa, situated near mount Sinai; his wife fell in labor and was delivered of a son, in a very dark and snowy night; he had also lost his way, and his cattle was scattered from him, when on a sudden he saw a fire by the side of a mountain, which on his nearer approach he found burning in a *green bush*. The Koran (chap. XX, vv. 9–14) says: "When he saw fire and said to his family: Tarry ye here, for I perceive fire: peradventure I may bring you a brand thereout, or may find a direction in our way by the fire. And when he was come near unto it, a voice called unto him, saying: O Moses! verily I am thy Lord: wherefore put off thy shoes: for thou art in the sacred valley Towa. And I have chosen thee: therefore hearken with attention unto that which is revealed unto thee. Verily I am God; there is no God beside me: wherefore worship me, and perform thy prayer in remembrance of me".

[1] The name of Pharâoh occurs several times in this work; but the character of this personage is viewed in a different light by the sectarians of Muhammedism. In the Koran he appears nearly as in the Bible of the Jews, with regard to Moses and the Israelites, cruel, tyrannical, presumptuous, and perishing in the Red Sea: not without having before acknowledged their God, and confessed his sins. But some Súfis see and admire in the impious daring of Pharâoh the omnipotence of his power, and adduce, in favor of their opinion, passages from some of their most celebrated philosophers. Indeed Jelaleddin represents Pharâoh equal to Moses. Sahel Ibn Abd-ullah of Shostr says, that the secret of the soul was first revealed when Pharâoh declared himself a God. Ghazáli sees in his temerity nothing else but the most noble aspiration to the divine, innate in the human mind.

that account the lord Imám Múheddín Shaikh Mahíeddín, in some of his compositions, exhibited proofs of Pharâoh's religion, and rendered this personage illustrious. Moses saw God under a bodily form, and did not find himself like that (exalted) being; but it was under his own form that Pharâoh saw God, and found himself like that being. Jesus declared himself the son of God; because he found himself the son of God Almighty, in a like manifestation.

Hajab, "the veil",[1] is of two kinds: the one, of darkness, is that of a servant, like morality and exterior occupations; and the other is the veil of light which comes from God; because traditions are veils of actions; actions, veils of attributes; and attributes, veils of the essence of revelation, which relates to mystery, dependent either upon exterior form or inner sense. The first kind of truth is called *Kashef surí*, the "exterior revelation"; the second kind is the *Kashef mâní*, "inner revelation". The exterior revelation takes place by means of sight, hearing, touch, smell, or rapture, and is dependent upon temporal traditions; this is called *rahbániyet,* "way-guarding", because the finding of truth according to investigation is contemplation, and some reckon this investigation among the sorts

---

[1] The Súfis call حجاب "veil", whatever is opposed to perfect union with divinity. In the life of *Joneid Abú'l-Kasem*, who was born and educated in Baghdád, and died in the year of the Hejira 297 (A.D. 909), one of the earliest and most celebrated founders of Súfism, we read what follows: "Somebody said to Joneid: 'I found that the Shaikhs of Khorasan acknowledge three sorts of veils: the first is the nature (of man); the second is the world, and the third concupiscence'. — 'These are', said Joneid, 'the veils which apply themselves to the heart of the common among men; but there exists another sort of veil for special men; that is, for the disciples of spiritual life, the Súfis: this is the view of works, the consideration of the recompenses due to acts, and the regard of the benefits of God. The Shaikh of Islamism said (relatively to this subject): God is veiled from the heart of man, who sees his proper actions; God is veiled even from him who seeks recompense, and from him who, occupied with considering the benefit, turns his eyes from the benefactor'." — (See *Notices et Extraits des MSS.*, vol. XII; p. 435, Joneid's Life, by Jámi, translated by Silvestre de Sacy.)

of *istidráj*,[1] "miracles permitted by God for hardening the hearts of sinners", and of *makr Ilahí*, "divine fascination".

Some derived the commands relative to the other world from the revelation, and confined their desires to *faná*, "annihilation", and *baká*, "eternal life". The author of this book heard from Sabjana that the exterior revelation concerning temporal actions is called "monastic institution",[2] because monks belong to the exterior people; and its worship is, according to rules, relative to every thing exterior; and its purpose, on account of service, directed to the retribution of deeds, reward of heaven, adherence to a particular prophet, and the like. Further obedience is an indication which bears towards temporal actions; on that account its revelation is connected with temporal concerns. The devout Muselman follows also the rule of monastic life, and the Christian is not without participation in absorption and eternal life.

It is to be known that in the service of a king there are two confidential Amirs, who are not friends, but entertain enmity against each other. They may bring their own friends before the king. So are the prophets appointed at the court *of God*; if not so, how would the

---

[1] استدراج is also interpreted: "prodigy of chastisement", that is, extraordinary things may be operated by a man who renounced obedience to God, in order that such a man may be led to perdition. This appears founded upon a passage of the Koran (chap. XVIII, vv. 43, 44): "Let me alone with him who accuseth this new revelation of imposture. We will lead them gradually to destruction by ways which they know not; and I will bear with them for a long time, for my stratagem is effectual".

[2] Monachism was not only disapproved but positively prohibited by the Muhammedan religion, the first founders of which, chiefs of warlike tribes, were by necessity, profession, and habit, continually engaged in military expeditions. But to the Asiatic, in general, so natural is asceticism, seclusion, and contemplation, that Muhammed, in order to restrain a propensity which he felt and now and then showed himself, declared that, for monachism, the pilgrimage to Mecca was substituted by divine order. Even during the prophet's life, the love of monastic and anachoretic professions gained ascendancy among Muselmans, and easily united with Súfism.

absolute Being have divided the extent of his empire by religion, if this were to be confined to one person? Another opinion is that of a pious philosopher, who contemplates the light of God in all objects of this and the other world, and turns not his regard from the least atom; he raised this belief to a high estimation; and to him remained no rancor of creed or religion; whoever, in the service of faith and morality is not freed from duality, and whoever says, the state of Muselmans is in dignity higher than that of Christians, knows nothing of the real Being. Whoever said of himself: "I attained a height of knowledge equal to that of *Mâruf Kerkhi*, said nothing else than this: the variety and multitude of the rules of prophets proceed only from the abundance of names, and, as in names there is no mutual opposition or contradiction, the superiority in rank among them is only the predominance of a name".

The Súfis say: The spirits of the perfect men[1] after separation from their bodies, go to the world of angels. The saints are directed by the interpretation of the

---

[1] نفوس كامله انسانى *nafus Kamilah insáni. Insan kamil*, "the perfect man", according to the doctrine of the Súfis, is, "the reunion of all the worlds, divine and natural, universal and partial; he is the book in which all books, divine and natural, are reunited. On account of his spirit and intellect, it is a reasonable book, called 'the Mother of Books'; on account of his heart, it is the book of the well-guarded table (*al lowh*); on account of his soul, it is the book of things obliterated and of things written; it is he who is then the venerable sublime and pure pages, which are not to be touched, and the mysteries which cannot be comprehended but by those who are purified from the dark veils. The relation of the first intelligence to the great world, and to its realities themselves, is as the relation of the human soul to the body and its faculties; for the universal soul is the heart of the great world, as the reasonable soul is the heart of the man, and it is on that account that the world is called 'the great Man'." — (*Definitions de Jorjani. Not. et Ext. des MSS.*, vol. IX, pp. 86–87.) In the passage just quoted, Silvestre de Sacy thinks *the perfect man* is equal to the first intelligence. – *The book of things obliterated and of things written*, the world of transitory things, in which life and death succeed each other. — *The universal soul* is an emanation of the divinity, subordinate to the first and universal intelligence.

Korán, and the vulgar people by the commentary upon both. Some maintain that the Saints do not subject themselves to it, but are tenacious only of this verse:

"Adore God, thy Lord, until attaining certitude (himself)".

The Shaikh Nájem eddin Kabra[1] said: When distinguished persons abandon the ceremonies of the worship, this means that these ceremonies which are performed by prescription, are contrary to them, because in worship no difficulty or inconvenience is to take place, but only joy and pleasure to be derived from it.

The lord Saíd Muhammed Nurbakhsh says, in the account of apparitions: The difference between *baroz*, "apparition", and *tanásokh*, "transmigration", is this: that the latter is the arrival of the soul, when it has separated from one body to take possession of another, in the embryo which is fit for receiving a soul in the fourth month, to be reckoned from the moment when the sperma fell and settled in the womb; and this separation from one body and junction with another is called *maâd*, "resurrection". An "apparition" is when a soul accumulates excellence upon excellence and an overflow takes place; so that by beatific vision it becomes visible; that is, it may happen, that a perfect soul, after its separation from the body, resides years in the upper world, and afterwards, for the sake of perfecting mankind, joins with a body, and the time of this junction is also the fourth month to be reckoned from the moment of the formation of the body, as was said upon transmigration.

It is stated, in the abridged commentary upon Gulshen-raz, that the soul cannot be without a body. When it is separated from the elemental body, it becomes a shadowy figure in the *barzakh*, that is, in the interval of time between the death and the resurrection of a man;[2]

---

[1] *Najem-eddin Abu 'l-Jenab Ahmed*, son of *Omar*, was a celebrated Súfi, who formed a great number of disciples. He was surnamed *Kobra*, "great", on account of his superior knowledge. He died in the year of the Hejira 618 (A.D. 1221).

[2] See page 45, note 1.

this is called "the acquired body". The barzakh, to which the soul is transported after its separation from this world, is another place than that which is between the spirits and the bodies. The first is called *ghaib imkaní*, "the possible disappearance", and the second *ghaib maháli*, "the illusive disappearance". All those who experience the possible disappearance, become informed of future events. There are many contradictory opinions about the illusive disappearance, which is the annunciation of the tidings of an extraordinary death. The lord Shaikh Muhammed Láhejí stated, in his commentary upon Gulshen-raz, that in the histories and accounts before-said is to be found, that *Jábilká* is a town of immense magnitude in the East, and *Jábilsá* a town of the utmost extent in the West, opposite to the former.[1] Commentators have said a great deal upon both. According to the impression which I, an humble person, have received upon my mind relative to this subject, without copying others, and conformably with the indications, there are two places; the one, *Jábilká* is *âalemimisal*, "the world of images", because on the east side the spirits emerge into existence. Barzakh (another name for it) is between the invisible and the visible, and contains every image of the world; certainly there may be a town of immense greatness, and *Jábilsá* is "the world of similitude". Barzakh is there the world in which the souls reside after their separation from the worldly station, all suitably to their deeds, manners, and words, good or bad, which they had made their own in the worldly station, as is to be found in the sacred verses and traditions. This Barzakh is on the west side of the material world, and is certainly a town of immense greatness, and opposite to it is Jábilká. The inhabitants of this town are gentle and just, whilst the people of Jábilsá, on account of the wicked deeds and manners which

[1] Jabilka and Jabilsa signify the double celestial Jerusalem of the Súfis: the first is the world of ideals, which is the wall of separation between the real and the mystic world; the second is the world of spirits after the completion of their career upon earth. — (See Von Hammer's *Gulshenraz*, p. 25.)

they had made their own in the worldly station, well deserve to be distinguished by the title of oppressors. Many entertain the opinion that both Barzakhs are but one; it should however be stated, that Barzakh in which the souls will abide after their separation from the worldly station is to the right of that Barzakh which is placed between the pure spirits and the bodies: because the gradations of the descent and ascent of beings form a circle, in which the junction of the last with the first point cannot be imagined but in the movement of the circle, and that Barzakh which is prior to the worldly station, with regard to the graduated descent, has a connection with the anterior worldly station; and that Barzakh, which is posterior to the worldly station, with regard to the graduated ascent, has a connection with the posterior worldly station. Further, whatever be the form of manners of the souls in the posterior Barzakh, this will also be the form of deeds, consequences of manners, actions, and qualities which had been owned in the worldly station, in opposition to the former Barzakh. Then the one is a stranger to the other; however, as both worlds, inasmuch as spiritual essences of light, being different from matter, are comprised in the visionary forms of the universe, they may be taken for synonymous. The Shaikh Dáúd Káíśerí relates that Shaikh Mahi-eddin of Arabia (may his tomb be purified!) has stated in the *Fatúhál*, "revelations", that *Barzakh* is different from the first; and the reason that the first is distinguished by the name of "possible absence", and the latter by "illusive absence", is, that every form in the first Barzakh is contingent, and depends upon exterior evidence, and every form in the last Barzakh, is inaccessible *to the senses*, and admits of no evidence but on the last day of the world. There are many expounders to whom the form of the first Barzakh appears evident, and who know what takes place in the world of accidents; however, few of these expounders are informed of the news of death.

The author of this book heard from Sabjáni, the learned in the knowledge of God; that the belief of the pure Súfis is the same as that of the *Ashrákían*, "the

Platonists"; but the Súfis have now mixed their creed with so many glosses, that nobody finds therein the door to the rules of the prophet, and the ancient Saints. Sabjáni gave the information that the essence of God Almighty is absolute light, absolute brightness, and mysterious life; that he is pure, and free from all colors, figures, shapes, and without a prototype; that the interpretation of the eloquent and the indications of the learned are deficient in the account of that light which is without color and mark; that the understanding of the learned and the wisdom of the sage is too weak for entirely comprehending the pure essence of that light, and as, conformably to these words:

"I was a hidden treasure; but I wished to be known, and I created the world for being known".

The essence of God the most High and Almighty showed his existence, so that, except him, there is no real being. In this employment of manifestation, he entered into contemplation, whence the sage calls him the first intelligence; because this lord of expansive creation considered every being according to the scope of propriety; and when the Almighty Being of expansive creation had examined every form inasmuch as by his power it was possible that such a form might appear, he fixed his contemplation in this employment of manifestation, so that what is called "the perfect spirit" is nothing else but himself. From Sabjani the information has been received and found in books that Abul Hassen Surí said: God Almighty rendered his spirit beauteous, then called it "truth", and made revelations, and brought forth names to the creatures; the absolute being has two heads: the first is *itlák sarf*,[1] "absolute excellence", and *vahedet mahs*,[2] "unmixed unity"; the second is *mukayed va kasret va badáyet*,[3] "compass, abundance, and primitiveness". This, according to the greatest number, relates to unity.

[1] .اطلاق صرف
[2] .وحدت محض
[3] .مقید و کثرت و بدایت

Further is *âkl-kulli*,[1] "the universal spirit", which incloses all realities which are (as it were) concrete in him, and this is called *ârsh-i-majíd*,[2] "the throne of glory" (the ninth or empyrean heaven); he is the truth of mankind, and between him and the majesty of divinity there is no mediator according to the wise, although some admit a difference. Sabjání said, this indicates that they wish no separation from the Lord of grace may ever take place. Moreover, the universal spirit, which embraces all realities in the way of expansion, they call *ârsh-i-Kerim*,[3] "the throne of mercy", and *lawh-i-mahfúz*,[4] "the tables of destiny". Besides, there is the universal nature, penetrating all material and spiritual beings, and this is called *âikâb*,[5] "vicissitude". With the philosophers nature is the noble part of bodies, and Sabjani stated, the penetrating nature in spirits indicates and signifies that there is one divine Being, and the rest nothing else but shadows. Finally, there is an essence of life, which the philosophers call *hayúli*, "the first principle of every thing material", and the Súfis call it *enka*.

SECTION III. – OF SOME OF THE SAINTS AMONG THE MODERNS, AND OF THE SUFIS, WHOM THE AUTHOR OF THIS WORK HAS KNOWN

The God-devoted lord Mawláná shah Badakhshí, when he had come from his accustomed abode to India, by the assistance of God was received among the disciples of Shah Mír of the Kádarí lineage, who had chosen his residence in the royal capital of Lahore, and acquired

[1] .عقل كلي
[2] .عرش مجيد
[3] .عرش كريم
[4] .لوح محفوظ
[5] .عقاب

great knowledge by his studies. From the original compositions of this sect of holiness, we have the following quatrain:

"The being who descended from his high sphere of sanctity,
From the absolute world, inclined towards the nether bondage,
He will, as long as the Lord forms mankind,
Remain fitted to the four elements".

Besides, the lord Mahi eddin Muhammed, the master of rank and dignity, the lord of the universe Dáráshukó,[1]

[1] Darashiko was the eldest son and heir presumptive of *Shah-Jehan*, of Delhi, during whose life he defended him against the rebellion of his younger brother, *Aureng-zeb*, who, leagued with two other brothers, attempted to dethrone his father. Dara, having been defeated in a battle on the river Jambul, retired towards Lahore, whilst the victorious Aureng-zeb proceeded to Agra, and by stratagem rendered himself master of his father's person, and imprisoned his brother Murad bakhsh, whom he had, till then, treated as emperor, in the castle of Agra, where the captive prince died. Proclaimed emperor under the title of *Aalemgir*, the new sovereign now turned his arms against Dara, who was in possession of the *Panj-ab, Multan*, and *Kabul*, and defended the line of the *Setlej*. Here beaten, Dara retired beyond the Indus, and took refuge in the mountains of Bikker. Aalumgir was called to *Allahabad*, to encounter his brother *Suja*, who had moved from Bengal to assert his right to the throne. Aalemgir had scarce repulsed him, when he was obliged to haste towards Guzerat: there was Dara, who had recrossed the Indus and taken an advantageous position in that maritime province. He might have been victorious in a battle, but he succumbed to the artfulness of Aalemgir. Deserted by his army, abandoned by his allies, he was delivered up by traitors to his cruel brother, subjected to an ignominious exposition in the streets of Delhi, and executed. Suja, Alemgir's last brother, was obliged to fly to Arrakan, where he died, seven years before his father, Shah Jehan, who died his son's prisoner, in 1665. I have related the principal events of one single year, 1658 of our era. This is a date in the life of the author of the Dabistán, then in his fortieth year or thereabout. He was before this time in the Panjab, and might have personally known Darashuko, who was renowned for his great learning and most religious turn of mind. Besides what is said above in our text, we know (see *Mémoires sur les particularités de la Religion musulmane*, par M. Garcin de Tassy, p. 107), that Dara frequented *Baba Lal*, a Hindu Durvish, who inhabited Dhianpur in the province

having, according to his desire, hastened to wait on his person, obtained the object of his wish, so that, whatever was established as certainty among the theological propositions which he found for the benefit of the travellers in the vast desert, he sent it to Kachmír, where the lord Múláná sháh keeps his residence.

"Upon the whole, God spoke by the tongue of Omar".

Any questions of every one who interrogates are asked from *him*, although they may fall from the tongue of the asker, and the hearing of every thing solicited comes from the asker, although he himself may not know it.

"All beings are one".

Some of this sect of Alides (may God sanctify their tombs!) also believe that the progress of perfection has no limits, because revelation is without limit, as it takes place every moment; hence it follows that the increase cannot be limited. So they say, if the Súfi live one thousand years, he still is in progress. Some of the ancient Shaikhs proffer, as a confirmation of this statement, that the Shaikh al islam, "the shaikh of the right faith", said: There exists no more evident sign of bad fortune than the day of a fixed fortune; whoever does not proceed, retrogrades. It is reported as the saying of the prophet (may the benediction of the most High be upon him):

"He whose two days are alike is deceived".

It was also said: "A traveller, who during two days goes on in the same manner, is in the way of detriment; he must be intent upon acquiring and preserving".[1]

The greatest part of this sect maintain the same

of Lahore, and conversed with him upon religious matters. The Munshi *Shanderban Shah Jehani* wrote a Persian work, which contains the pious conversations of these personages.

---

[1] These are evidently sentiments conducive to progressive civilization and perfection of mankind, and prove that, in Asia, even under the domination of the Muhammedan religion, men felt that they are not doomed to be *stationary*; thus the absurd dogma of fatality was, by a fortunate inconsistency, counterbalanced by the dictates of sound reason. Unfortunately, our author, generally so liberal-minded, appears upon that point not to range himself upon the most rational side.

doctrine, but, by the benediction of my Shaikh, the crier for help in the quarters of heaven, the teacher of the people of God, the godly, the lord Mulána Shah (the peace and mercy of God be his!), upon me, an humble person, fell, as if it were the splendor of the sun, and made it clear to me that the Súfi has degrees and a limit of perfection, that, after having attained it, he remains at that height; because with me, an humble broken individual, to remain at a height attained, is proficiency, inasmuch as every state has its perfection, and the perfection of a progressing state annihilates the progress. This is also the meaning of the before-quoted saying of the prophet; because there is absolute freedom with those only who are united with bondage with those who tend towards God, and absorb him, and the words "two days" refer to time. In the same manner my master (the mercy of God be upon him!) interpreted those words. The truth is, that they have not understood the saying, and have not penetrated into the interior sense of the figurative expression: because the latter refers in truth to the insufficiency of a contemplative man. And this sense agrees with that of the following authentic tradition of the prophet (the peace and blessing of the Highest be upon him):

> "There are moments in which I am with God in such a manner that neither angel nor arch-angel, nor prophet, nor apostle, can attain to it".

These words confirm his having once been in a lower station. It is said that the prophet (the peace and blessing of the most High be upon him!) was not always of the same disposition, the same state, and the same sort of constitution; but this is not so, but from the same approved tradition it is evident that the prophet (peace and blessing upon him!) was always in the same state, and no ascent nor descent was possible therein; because he says: "Yon place was at once so contiguous to me, that no cherub or no divine missioned prophet ever found himself in such a situation". The time of a prophet is a universal one, and is free from temporariness: this time has neither priority nor posteriority —

"With thy Lord there is neither morning nor evening".

Except this, the noble tradition has no meaning, which is also evident from the obvious interpretation, and moreover included in the state of perfection and constitution of Muhammed (peace and blessing upon him!). But, in the sense which they attribute to the words, a deficiency is necessarily implied. The state of the lord of the world (Muhammed) is always in the perfection of unity; this is the best to adopt, at times in a particular, and at times in a general qualification. There is also another interpretation which the Shaikhs (the mercy of the most High be upon them) gave to these words: inasmuch as the gradations of these Saints are infinite. Thus in the work *Nefhât ul ins*, "the fragrant gales of mankind",[1] the opinion of the Shaikhs is stated to be, that some of the saints are without a mark and without an attribute, and the perfection of a state, and the utmost degree to which Saints may attain, is to be without an attribute and without a mark. It was said:

"He who has no mark, his mark are we".

Besides, those who acknowledge an ascent without a limit, if in the pure being and true essence of the glorious and most high God, who is exempt and free from ascent and descent, color, odor, outwardness and inwardness, increase and decrease, they admit a progression, it must also be admissible in the existence of a Súfi professing the unity of God. And if they do not admit a gradation of progress *in God*, then they ought not to admit it in the professor of the divine unity, who in the exalted state of purity and holiness became united with him. When a devotee among men, having left the connexion with works of supererogation, arrives at that of divine precepts, he realises the words:

"When thou didst cast thy arrows against them, thou didst not cast them, but God slew them".[1]

---

[1] This is a work of the celebrated Abd-al rahmen Jámi.

[2] Koran, chap. VIII, v. 17. We have mentioned Muhammed's victory gained at Bedr over a superior force of the Koreish. The prophet, by the direction of the angel Gabriel, took a handful of

It may be said: Certainly, he who became one with God, and of whose being not an atom remained, he, from whose sight both worlds vanished, who in the steps of right faith arrived at the rank of perfect purity, and from truth to truth became God, what then higher than God can there ever be, to which the pious professor of unity may further tend to ascend? It is known:

"Beyond blackness, no color can go".[1]

Every one, as long as he is in the state of progress, cannot have arrived at the condition

"Where there is no fear and no care".

Because care and fear derive from ascent and descent. Fear at ascending is in the expectation whether the ascent will succeed or not, but whoever disregards ascent and descent, and elevates himself above care and fear, he

gravel, and threw it towards the enemy, saying: "May their faces be confounded": whereupon they immediately turned their backs and fled. Hence the above passage is also rendered: "Neither didst thou, O *Muhammed!* cast *the gravel into their eyes*, when thou didst *seem to* cast *it*, but God cast *it*".

[1] The assumption of being God was not uncommon among the Súfis. One of the most distinguished was *Hassain Manśur Hallaj*, a disciple of Joneid. After having taught the most exalted mysticism, in several countries, Hallaj was condemned to death in Baghdad, according to Ben Shohnah on account of a point of his doctrine concerning the pilgrimage to Mecca, for which he thought some other good works might be justly substituted, according to Sheheristáni and others, on account of having proclaimed himself to be God. During the infliction of one thousand stripes, followed by a gradual dismemberment of his whole body, he never ceased, by words and acts, to give demonstrations of the most ecstatic joy. The manner of his death is variously related. — (See Herbelot, and *Taskirat al aulia*, by Farid-eddin in Tholuck's *Blüthen sammlung aus morgenländischer Mystik, S.* 311–327.) Abu Yezid Bastami (before mentioned, p. 33, note) also used to salute himself as God. "Agriculturists", says Ghazali, "left their fields and assumed such a character; nature is delighted with speeches which permit works to be neglected, under the illusion of purifying the heart by the attainment of certain degrees and qualities". This opinion produced great evils, "so that", adds the said author in his indignation, "to put to death the lowest of those who set forth such futile pretensions, is more consistent with God's religion than to preserve the life of ten persons". — (See Pocock, first edit., pp. 268–269.)

obtains tranquillity in tranquillity, and rectitude in rectitude. And the verse of the merciful is:

"Keep thyself upright as thou wast directed".

Hence is also understood, that the Súfi remains steadfast in the dignity of perfection, for rectitude is perseverance. O Muhammed! it is necessary; remain fixed in the dignity of professing the unity of God, which is free from the misfortune of inconstancy. And the verse of the merciful is:

"The day on which I perfected religion for your sake, and rendered complete my favor towards you".

This indicates clearly the meaning that, by this perfection also, the prophet (upon whom be the peace and the blessing of the most High!) is manifested. And those who, on account of the infinity of revelation, hold progress to be perpetual, are not right: because, as long as the sight is illuminated by the light of the revelation, the revelationists and the illuminated are still separate, and not yet become one:[1] in this state there is duality and infidelity in the individual who has not yet been liberated from the idea of something double in himself, and he to whom an atom of something else but that one remains

---

[1] As long as the Sufi is conscious of the least distinction between God and himself, he is not thoroughly penetrated by the unity of God. Here follows the translation of a passage taken from the Masnavi of the celebrated Jelal eddin Rumí, which passage, we may agree with Silvestre de Sacy, admirably expresses this mystic doctrine in the form of an apologue: "A man knocked at the door of his friend. The latter asked: 'Who art thou, my dear?' — 'It is I'. — 'In this case, be off; I cannot at present receive thee; there is no place at my board for one who is still *raw*; such a man cannot be sufficiently *dressed* (that is matured) and cured of hypocrisy, but by the fire of separation and refusal'. The unfortunate man departed. He employed a whole year in travelling, consuming himself in the flames of desire and affliction, caused by the absence of his friend. Matured and perfected by his long trial, he again approached the door of his friend and knocked modestly, fearful that an uncivil word might again fall from his own lips. — 'Who is there?' was asked from the interior of the house'. — 'Dear friend, it is thyself who art at the door'. — 'Because it is myself, enter to-day; this house can contain no other than I'." — (See *Notices et Extraits des MSS.*, vol. XII, pp. 430–431, note 4.)

attached is reckoned, by all professors of unity and by all perfect saints, to be one who gives partners to God or an infidel, and in a state of deficiency.

"It behoves thee to keep neither soul nor body,
And if they both remain, I do not remain;
As long as a hair of thee remains upon its place,
Know, by this one hair, thy foot remains fettered.
As long as thou playest not at once thy life,
I shall consider thee as polluted and impious".

* Why dost thou not thyself produce revelation, so that thou mayest always be illuminated? *

As this question, solved in this manner by me, humble individual, was very abstruse, I sent it to my friends, that, if there were occasion for *further* discussion, they might write to me, and thus the matter be better elucidated. God alone is all-sufficient; the rest is inordinate desire. What has been hitherto said is taken from the prince of the world (Dara sheko).

It should be known that, in the work *Merás ed al ânáyet*, "Observations upon the blessed favor", is stated, that the sect, which in their (exalted) feeling[1] conquer the state of *jazbet*,[2] *jamâ va vahedet*, "attraction, union, and unity", have acquired, by means of the superiority of the manifest name (*the quality of*) exterior deity, and interior and hidden creation. This sect is called, in the language of the Súfis, *saheban-i-kereb*[3]*-i-ferâis*, "the masters of prox-

* The words between asterisks are not joined in the text to the verses; they seem nevertheless to belong to them, although not in the metre of the other lines.

[1] مذاق , "tasting", from ذوق , *zawk*, "taste, delight", is above employed in a wide acceptation, and means in the technical language of the Súfis an uncommon exaltation of the mind.

[2] جذبه , "attraction", is a mystical state, in which God attracts the saint, in order that he, an obedient servant, may direct his mind towards the side to which he is attracted, and may be inflamed in such a manner as to rise up towards heaven. The *majezub*, "attracted", form a particular class of the Súfis. — (See pp. 47–49, note 1.)

[3] قرب , "proximity", a technical term of the Súfis, is referred to

imity to divine precepts", and this proximity is acknowledged to be that of divine precepts. This sect, which, on account of the proper meaning of the name of *al báten*, "interior", may be brought into relation with expansive creation and hidden reality, this sect after *jamâ*, "union", obtains *ferk*, "division",[1] and this is called *kereb-i-navâfil*, "proximity of supererogation". The lord Shaikh Muhammed Láheji stated that *jamâ*, "union", is contrary to *ferk*, "division"; and division is the veil of God before the creatures. Every one sees the creation, but acknowledges God to be without it; every one has the sight of God by means of the creation, that is, every one sees God, but the creation by itself affords no access to the sight of him.

Besides, the Mariyam of the world, the Fátima of the time and ages, the purity of human kind, the protecting intelligence, *Jehán ára* "the ornament of the world", the *begum*, the lady, the daughter of *Abu 'l Muzafer Shíhábu 'd dín Muhammed sáhib-Kirán sání Amir ul muslemin sháh Jehán pádsháh ghází*, "the victorious lord, the bright star of religion, Muhammed, a second Sáhib Kírán, the Amir of the believers, Shah Jehan, the conquering emperor", having secretly followed, by the desire of her heart, the

---

[1] جمع and فرق are terms used in a particular sense by the Sufis. In the state of *Jamâ*, "union", the mystic sees but God and his unity; in the state of *ferk*, "division", man enters again into the natural state, and occupies himself with good works and the fulfilment of precepts. He does even what is not prescribed conformably with this passage of the Koran (chap. XVII, v. 81): "Watch some part of the night in the same exercise (praying), as a work of supererogation for thee; peradventure thy Lord will raise thee to an honorable station". These two states (union and division) are necessary to the mystic. The following passage of the Koran is quoted as an authority for this doctrine: *God testifies that there is no God but him*; this is "union"; *and the angels testify the same, as well as the men who possess the science*; this is "division".

the words addressed by God to Muhammed: "adore and approach". A man approaches God by all acts which may procure him happiness, and it is not God who approaches man, because God is always near all men, whether they be predestined to heaven or hell; but it is man who approaches God.

injunctions of the blessed Mullá shah, turned her face to the right rule, and attained her wish, the full knowledge of God. One of the wonderful speeches of this blessed and exalted personage, whom the author of this book knew, is the following: In the year of the Hejira 1057 (A.D. 1647) Mulla shah came to the house of a friend in Hyderábád. One of the persons present, by way of reproving allusion, began to ask questions about the hurt which the bégum of the lord received by fire. The teacher of morality said to him: "A slight garment imbibed with oil, when it takes fire, is easily burnt"; in such a manner came the misfortune upon the most pure form of her majesty. This person laughed and continued to revile. By accident, somebody came from the house of this person and said: "What, art thou sitting here, whilst thy sister is burnt, because fire fell upon her garment". The master observed: "In such a manner, I said, befell misfortune on the illustrious princess; God has shown it to thee".

"The lamp which God has lighted,
Whoever blows it out burns his beard".

The Sufi Mulla Ismâíl Isfahaní, seeking enjoyment, came from Iran to the great towns of India, and in Lahore visited the lord Mián Mír; he chose the condition of a Durvish, and from Lahore soon betook himself to Kashmir, where he abandoned the worldly affairs, and practised pious austerity. The author of this book saw him in Kashmír, in the year of the Hejira 1049 (A.D. 1639). The following verse is by him:

"I knocked down every idol which was in my way,
No other idol remains to my veneration but God himself".

From Mírzá Muhammed Makím, the jeweller, the information was received that Mír Fakher eddin Muhammed Tafresí was occupied in Kashmir with reviling and reproving Mulla Ismâíl and Fakher, and said: "These belong to the infidels, and are destined to hell". Mulla Ismâíl answered: "In this state I withheld my hand from worldly affairs, and in this world never was associated to thee; in like manner in the future world, as, according to thy opinion, we are infidels, and go to hell, and not to heaven with thee; therefore it behoves thee to be satisfied and content with us, as we have left to thee the present and the future world. The Mobed says:

> "The pious and the idolaters are satisfied with us, as we
> Are not ourselves their partners, neither in this nor in the other world;
> Enmity arises from partnership; we, with the intention of friendship,
> Gave up the future, and follow the present world".

Mírzá Muhammed Mokim, the jeweller, further said: A person gave bad names to Fakheraye Fál; the latter, looking towards him, gave him no answer. When we asked him the reason of his silence, he replied: "A man moved his lips, and agitated the air; what does that concern me?" Fakher, the ornament of mankind, was not much addicted to religious austerity, but gave himself up to counselling, reforming, and correcting others. He assumed the surname of *Tarsa*, "timid, or unbeliever"; he called the Journal of his travels, *Dair-namah*, "Journal of a tavern (also monastery)". In this Journal are the following lines:

> "I met upon my road with a bitch,
> Like a dog guided by scent in the circle of a chase.
> Her paw was colored with blood,
> In the middle of the road she lay like a tiger;
> Impelled either by wild instinct or necessity,
> She had made her own whelp the aliment of life.
> At the sight of so strange a scene,
> I restrained my hand from striking, and opening my lips,
> I said: 'O dog, what desirest thou to do?
> Upon thy own heart why inflicting all this pain?'
> Scarce had the tip of my tongue perforated the pearl of the secret,
> When her tail was agitated, and she said:
> 'O thou who art not informed of thy own state,
> How shall I give thee an account of my condition?'
> When the words of the dog came upon my ear,
> A resplendent sun fell into my mind.
> In the sense of (*these words indicative of the dog's*) insanity,

My own sense found the authority of a precept.[1]
The desire of wandering in the garden left my heart,
Which assumed the quality of a tulip and a deep mark;
It saw nothing upon the path of profligacy
But the privation of remedies.
I said again to her: 'O lion-like dog,
The morning-breeze learns from thee rapidity:
Manifest to me the state of thy heart,
Exhibit to me the form of its history'.
She gave a howl, and, emitting lamentations,
Rendered testimony of her own secret condition:
'I devoured the blood of the offspring of my own womb
That nobody might place a weight upon my head'".

In the year of the Hejira 1056 (A.D. 1647), according to information received, Fakhera Tarsa left his old habitation in Ahmed ábad of Guzerat. The father of the Durvish, the pious Sabjáni, was an inhabitant of Hirát, but he was born in India. This illustrious person made a great proficiency in the sciences of philosophy and history, and acquired also a fortune; but he at last turned his face from it, and chose retirement and solitude; for many years he followed the footsteps of a perfect spiritual guide; he travelled to see monasteries and hermitages, until he became the disciple of Shaikh Mujed eddín Muhammed Balkhí Káderí, who was free, virtuous, and remote from the world. The said Shaikh read the whole work of Shaikh Mohí eddín Arabi before his master, and his master perused it likewise with Shaikh Sader eddin Kautíví, who had heard the whole of it from Shaikh Mohí eddín. The pious Sabjáni frequently expounded the words of the lord Rais ul Mohedín, "the chief of the believers of divine unity", Shaikh Mohí eddín Arabí, and those of the best Súfis, and as he was carried to the very limit of evidence, he found them conformable with the

[1] یافت دران مرغ زدیوانکــی
مرغ دلـم منصب پروانکــی

Literally: "In this bird from insanity the bird of my heart found the station of a command". It is known that *murgh*, "birds", among other significations, has that of "the heart, the understanding".

doctrine of the Platonists. The godly Sabjáni studied the whole work of the celebrated Shaikh in the service of his perfect master. After this attendance, having resigned every thing into the hands of the fortunate Shaikh, he turned his face entirely to sanctity, and lived a considerable time retired in solitude, until his master declared to him: Now, thou hast attained perfection. The pious Sabjáni keeps nothing with him but the cover of his privities; he abstains from eating the flesh of any animal; he asks for nothing; if any sustenance be left near him, provided it be not animal food, he takes a little of it; he venerates the mosques and the temples of idols; and he performs in *butgadah*,[1] "house of idols", according to the usage of the Hindus, the *puja* and *dandavet*, "worship and prostration", that is, the religious rites, but in the mosques he conforms in praying after the manner of the Muselmans; he never abuses the faith and rites of others; nor gives he one creed preference over another; he always practises abstinence, but at times he breaks the fast with some fruits from the mountains, such as pine-kernels, and the like; he takes no pleasure in demonstrations of honor and magnificence to him, nor is he afflicted by disdain and contempt, and in order to remain unknown to men, he dwells in the *Kohistan*, "mountainous country" of the Afgháns and Kafris, and the like. The Kafrís are a tribe from Kabulistan, and are called Kafer *Katóriz*, who before lived upon mountains, in deserts and forests, remote and concealed from others.

The author of this book saw Sabjáni in the year of the Hejira 1046 (A.D. 1636) in upper Bangash. This personage never sleeps at night, but sits awake in deep meditation; every one who sees him would take him for a divine being. Shaikh Sâdi says:

"Dost thou not know that, when I went to the friend,
As soon as I arrived before him, I said: 'It is he',"[2]

[1] *But-gadah* appears to me to have been corrupted into *pagoda*, the modern name of a Hindu temple in popular language. This name has also been derived from *bhagavata*, but, if I am not mistaken, with less probability.
[2] See page 77, note 1.

Sabjání appears a (divine) revelation in his actions, steps, attributes, and nature, and to have attained the summit of perfection. He said that, with respect to the other world, there are several classes of men. The one denies the absolute being; another interprets it in an abstract manner of reasoning, inasmuch as they have sufficient intelligence to be modest and conciliating. The distinguished Súfis, without interpreting the different systems of nations, which, in their separate creeds of various kinds and religions, differ about the beforesaid object, view in the bodies the agreeableness of imagery. Khiźer, Elías, Brahma, Ganésa, and all the gods of India, these and the like representations, which in this world have no reality, all are distinct objects of imagination. Essential is what was said by Abu Nazer Farábí (may God illume his grave!) that the common people view their creeds under the form of their imagination. The author of this book heard also from the lord, the pious Sabjání: The contemplative man sees every one whom he loves and esteems, frequently in dreams in a beautiful shape, and in an exalted state, although to other people he may appear iniquitous; and the person whom he knows to be depraved, will often be viewed by him in a repulsive condition, although to the crowd he may appear glorious and powerful. Hence follows, that the learned among the contemplative persons make use of a negative argument in their creed, in order that it may become evident what the truth really is. When any one sees a person of high rank, such as a prophet, an Imám, or any dignified individual, in a state of some deficiency, he views his own defects in his understanding, spirit, heart, or nature; and as these things are but seeming defects in the great personage, he must endeavor to remove them from himself. In like manner, if one sees a person in good health (appearing to him) in a state of illness, there is illness in his own state, and if he thinks him bad with regard to his own faith, he ought to be somewhat disposed to think that person good.

A disciple demanded some employment from Sabjání. The master asked him: "Hast thou devoted thyself to piety?" The answer was: "I have". Then Sabjání said: "If thou art a Muselman, go to the Franks, and stay with that people; if thou art a Nazarean, join the Jews; if a Sonni, betake thyself to Irak, and hear the speeches and reproaches of those men; if thou professest to be a Shíah, mix with the schismatics, and lend thy ear to their words; in this manner, what ever be thy religion, associate with men of an opposite persuasion; if, in hearing their discourses thou feelest but little disturbed, thy mind keeps the tenor of piety; but if thou art not in the least moved and mixest with them like milk and sugar, then certainly thou hast attained the highest degree of perfect peace, and art a master of the divine creation".

Yusef was a man belonging to the tribe of Durds,[1] and in his youth a hermit; at last, by his efforts, he found access to the intellectual world, and by the grace of God he carried it so far, that he was ranged among the disciples called Sanyásis, on account of their piety and knowledge, and among the learned followers of the celebrated master, who dwelt in Bárahmúlah, a village in Kachmir. It so happened that, when he devoted himself to his service, he found what he was in search of. Shaikh Atar says:

"An unbeliever becomes a relation by love;
A lover acquires the high sense of a durvish".

Having known many countries and persons, he became impressed with the marks of revelations. So it happened that the author of this book heard from him what follows: "One night I saw in a dream that the world was deluged by water; there remained no trace of a living being, and I was myself immersed in the water. In the midst of this state I saw a kingly rider come, sitting upon his horse upon the surface of the water. When he came near me, he said to me: 'Come with me that I may save thee'. I replied: 'Who art thou?' He answered: 'I am the self-existing being, and creator of all things'. Then I

---

[1] The Durds are the inhabitants of the mountainous country to the west of Kachmir.

began to follow him rapidly, and run along the surface of the water, until I arrived in a garden. There I put my foot on the ground, and, directing my sight to the right, I beheld a delightful spot, full of all sorts of odoriferous herbs and elevated palaces, huris (beautiful virgins), kaśurs (bridal chambers), and youths and boys, and all the gifts of heaven, as well as the blessed, occupied with enjoyments. Besides, at the left, I saw pits, black, narrow, and tenebrious; and therein, like bats, suspended a crowd of miserable beings whose hands and feet were tied to the neck. The horseman, after having invited me to a pleasure-walk in the garden, wanted to conduct me out of the delightful place, but I had resolved in myself that, like Idris, I would not go out of it. Then I stuck close to the door, and took fast hold of the post. When I awoke from sleep, I found my lips held fast by both my hands; and thus it was revealed to me that, whatever is, exists within mankind itself.

"Demand from thyself whatever thou wishest: for thou art every thing".

It is related: That there was a man called *Baháder* among the Hindus, and he happened to have no male offspring in his house; therefore he came to Baba Yúsef, and demanded his benediction. Baba Yúsef gave him a bit of white earth, and said to him: "Let thy wife eat it". When the man had done as was enjoined him, a boy was born in his house, and received the name of *Rahu*. This individual, by the favor of the friends of God, became a learned man, and acquired the surname of "independent", as was said in the chapter of the Jnanian.[1]

The Mulla, called Umer, prohibited Baba Yúsef to listen to music, and whatever gentle entreaties Baba Yúsef employed, he paid no attention to them; at last the Baba, in the perturbation of his mind, threw a small fragment of stone upon him, in such a manner that Mulla Umer lost his senses for some time; when he recovered, he prostrated himself before the Baba, went out, and was no more seen.

---

[1] We find nothing upon this Rahu in the preceding pages.

Yúsef, the inspired, was a durvish, devoted to the practice of restraining his breath, which he carried so far that he kept his breath during four watches (twelve hours).[1] One of his friends said to the author of this book in Kachmir, that Yúsef during a length of time ate nothing at all. The friend related: "I went one night to watch with him; he said to me: 'Go and eat something'. I replied: 'I will; but it would be well that thou also shouldst take something to eat and to drink'. His answer was: 'Thou art not able to satisfy my want of food'. I assured him: 'I am able'. He then ordered: 'Go, bring what thou hast'. I went home and brought him a great dish full of rice, a large cup of coagulated milk, with bread and other eatables, as much as might have been sufficient for ten gluttons; he eat up every thing, and said: 'Bring something more'. I went home, prepared a meal for twenty persons, and with the aid of the people of the house, brought it to him. He eat it up, and desired more. I returned home, and carried to him meats half cooked and other things. He eat up all, and said: 'Bring more'. I fell at his feet; he called out: 'Have I not said to thee that thou wouldst not be able to satisfy my want of food'."

One of his disciples related: Yúsef said, that he has seen God the Almighty in the shape of a man, sitting in his house. The author of this book frequented the society of many contemplative pious Súfis, and learned men of this sect, elevated in rank; if he should relate all he knows of them, he would have to write a copious work.

---

[1] The practice of holding the breath, often mentioned in this work, is founded upon the belief, that to each man a certain number of respirations is allotted: the less he breathes the longer he lives. — (Shakespear's Dictionary, p. 365.)